Marketing

CONTENTS

OUTLINE

This unit introduces the major principles which underpin marketing, namely the anticipation of market needs and opportunities; the satisfaction of consumer expectations; the maximisation of benefits to the organization, including income generation and/or profits; managing the effects of change and competition; the coordination of activities to achieve marketing aims; making use of technological developments; and enhancing the perception of the organization, product or service by consumers. Implementing these principles involves marketing research, effective communications, and sales and customer service. Each of these is the subject of an element in the unit.

Note: each of the Collins Educational Advanced GNVQ
Business Units have been published separately. Figures have
been numbered according to the Unit in which they appear.

Published by
Collins Educational Ltd
An imprint of HarperCollins *Publishers*
77–85 Fulham Palace Road
Hammersmith
London W6 8JB

First published 1995

ISBN 000322449X

Designed and edited by DSM Partnership.
Cover designed by Trevor Burrows.
Project managed by Patricia Briggs.
Printed and bound by Scotprint Ltd., Musselburgh, Scotland.

ACKNOWLEDGEMENTS
The author and publisher would like to thank the following for
permission to reproduce material:

Central Statistical Office for the following extracts from *Social
Trends 1994*: 'Household expenditure 1971-1992, selected items,
at constant (1990) prices' (p. 20); 'Households, by size, *per cents*
and totals, Great Britain' (p. 22); 'Ethnic groups, Great Britain,
1991' (p. 23); 'Participation in the most popular sports, games and
physical activities, by age, Great Britain, 1990' (p. 24); 'Savings, by
social class, age and sex, Great Britain, 1993' (p. 24); 'Readership
of national newspapers, by sex and age, Great Britain, 1992' (p.
35); 'Readership of the most popular magazines, by sex and age,
1992' (p. 36). Crown copyright 1994. Reproduced by the
permission of the Controller of HMSO and the Central Statistical
Office.

HI-TEC Sports UK for the case study material (pp. 14-6).

Marketing, 'The Packaging Prodigies', 20 January 1994 (pp. 7-8);
'Penguin Targets Kids', 17 February 1994 (p. 13); 'Research
Propels Innovation', 27 January 1994 (p. 18); 'Live Viewing', 1
December 1994 (p. 37-8); 'Maximising your Market Impact', 9
March 1995 (p. 41); Direct mail expenditure graph, 9 March
1995 (p. 43).

Newsweek, 'What matters to consumers?', 24 July 1995 (p. 23).

The Observer, 'Daewoo pronounces death of the salesman', 9
April 1995 (pp. 55-6).

The Voice, 'Soul-d on Healthy Food!', 11 July 1995 (p. 21).

Every effort has been made to contact copyright holders, but if
any have been inadvertently overlooked, the publishers will be
pleased to make the necessary arrangements at the first
opportunity.

Principles and functions of marketing

Marketing is the management process of identifying, anticipating and satisfying consumer requirements in such a way as to yield a profit, while also encouraging consumers to make further purchases and to recommend the products and services of the organisation.

This means that those responsible for marketing within an organisation need to be able to identify the needs of their potential customers. It is also necessary to be able to anticipate those future trends and developments which could influence the customer's requirements; for example, a furniture warehouse would need to increase its stock in anticipation of an upturn in the housing market.

Marketing also involves constantly reviewing all aspects of a product or service in order to ensure that it continues to satisfy the potential customer's requirements. This means having the right product or service, at the right price, and it being on sale at the right time and place. Only when all these factors have been satisfied is it likely that a private sector organisation will be able to make a profit or a public sector organisation or charity to be effective in meeting its objectives. Ultimately, an organisation can claim that its marketing is successful when consumers make repeat purchases or are prepared to make recommendations about the organisation's products or services.

OBJECTIVES

The primary aim of marketing is to ensure that consumers buy products or services. However, the ways in which marketing is carried out varies enormously between organisations according to their size and the nature of their products or services. In a small business, the marketing role may be carried out by a single person. Many sole traders have to make marketing decisions, along with other business decisions, in areas such as purchasing, production and finance. In the case of a one-person mobile hot dog stall, the owner has to purchase supplies and equipment, cook the product and control the financing of the operation, as well as make all the marketing decisions. These will include deciding on the most important features of the product for target consumers in terms of type and size of roll, sausage and sauces; how much should be charged; where the mobile unit should be located; and how the business should be promoted through, say, signs by the roadside or advertising.

In a much larger organisation there may be specialists responsible for each part of the marketing operation. *Fig 3.1* shows how marketing could be organised in a business which has markets at home and abroad.

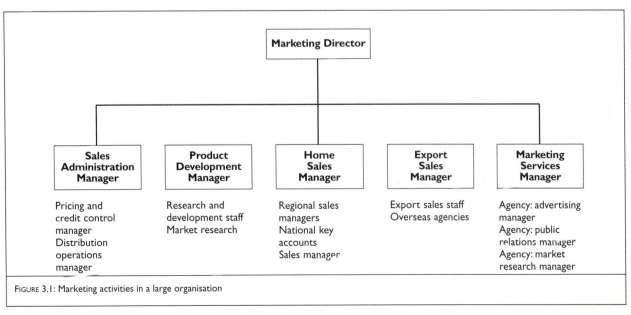

FIGURE 3.1: Marketing activities in a large organisation

The most important domestic customers would be handled by a special key account manager. Some of the work connected with market research, public relations and advertising could be handled by outside agencies.

Whatever the form of organisation of the marketing operation, it must be well coordinated and have well-defined lines of communication with other departments. If this is not the case, there is always a danger that problems will arise in terms of production, purchasing and finance. Costly errors may be made about levels of production and the purchasing of raw materials and components, upsetting financial planning.

The way in which marketing activities are carried out within an organisation varies according to whether it is **product-oriented** or customer-oriented. In the case of the former, there may be an assumption by those working in the organisation that the existing range of products or services is the best on the market and that sales will follow automatically, so there is no need for product change or modification. Such a complacent view can lead to the downfall of an organisation when it is operating in a rapidly changing business environment. For example, some companies producing towelling nappies were badly caught out by the introduction of the paper-based disposable nappy. A **customer-oriented** organisation, on the other hand, is in a constant state of change, assessing, monitoring and responding to changes in the market. It will have a highly developed marketing strategy, which acknowledges and is sensitive to its customers' changing needs and wants. It will strive to find out what customers want, what causes them to buy products, and what the product or service really means to them as consumers. From the top down, the organisation and all its decision makers will be market led, recognising that tomorrow's profitability depends upon meeting today's needs.

This means taking a 'whole company' approach towards marketing, as is demonstrated in the Kwik-Fit case study, below.

KWIK-FIT

From the very beginning, Kwik-Fit aimed to give its customers the benefits they really wanted – fast service, quality products and competitive prices.

Chairman Tom Farmer says that success is due to getting results in five key areas, called 'The Kwik-Fit System'. The system highlights several aspects of good marketing practice: identifying and responding to current and future motoring needs; developing specialist repair and replacement outfits; well-trained and highly-motivated staff; sophisticated computer systems and management support; and a distinctive and high-profile brand image.

Kwik-Fit's ability to identify and exploit trends in its markets is illustrated by its Child Safety Scheme, encouraging the fitting of child safety seats in cars and, more recently, the supply of child cycle helmets.

Staff training receives considerable investment – £2.5m last year. All service centre staff are trained in customer service as well as technical skills. The bold claim, 'You can't get better than a Kwik-Fit fitter', is deliberately made to give staff something to live up to. It's not just a TV advertising slogan, it's emblazoned on the overalls of staff. 'To the public, "You can't get better than a Kwik-Fit fitter" is an advertising slogan,' says Tom Farmer. 'To us, it's a philosophy.'

The customer, however, remains at the centre of the company's focus. To quote Tom Farmer: 'We aren't interested in satisfied customers. We want delighted customers.'

From: *Marketing: the way forward*, Department of Trade and Industry, 1992

Within the customer-oriented organisation, marketing features prominently in overall planning. Any market plan will be based on the strategic plan of the organisation and will be run and controlled by the systems operating within the organisation. Consequently, the objectives behind marketing activities are determined by the overall objectives of the business organisation of which there may be several (see *Fig 3.2*).

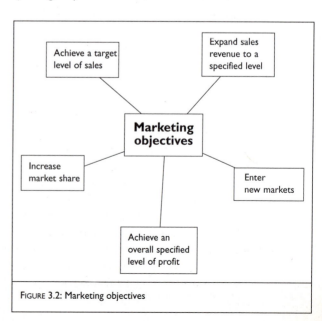

FIGURE 3.2: Marketing objectives

Unfortunately, both marketing and strategic objectives may conflict with the needs of customers, who generally want:

⊗ **high-quality goods and services;**

⊗ **low prices;**

⊗ **an adequate choice;**

⊗ **an efficient and convenient system of distribution;**

⊗ **imaginatively presented and detailed information about the products and services; and**

⊗ **a rapid response to any changes in technology.**

Many of these factors are quite expensive to provide in terms of changes in an organisation's production methods and standards of service and this may have an adverse effect on the organisation's ability to maintain its productivity and, ultimately, its profitability.

In order to achieve its overall objectives, a non-profit making organisation, such as a charity or voluntary body, also has to pay attention to marketing and the achievement of high standards of customer (or member) care. For example, in 1994, the Royal Society for the Protection of Birds (RSPB) had a total income of over £30m and membership of around one million. The major objective of the RSPB is the conservation of wild birds and the preservation of the environment on which they depend. This involves the organisation in six major activities: research, education, advice, campaigning, the management of nature reserves and specific measures to protect birds. The RSPB's success in these areas depends on its ability to market itself in order to attract income from membership subscriptions, legacies, fundraising, business support, charitable trusts, films, consultancy, grants and rents. This can only be achieved by the organisation being member-oriented, constantly monitoring and reflecting members' needs in terms of the facilities available on nature reserves, the types of publications and films produced, and by setting the membership fee at a level sufficient both to provide the required income and to sustain membership numbers.

ACTIVITY

McFacts

⊗ McDonald's has over 16,000 restaurants in at least 83 countries, serving more than 28 million people each day.

⊗ There are more than 600 McDonald's restaurants in the United Kingdom, serving 1.5m customers each day. The number of restaurants is expected to double by the end of the year 2000.

⊗ McDonald's UK sales in 1994 were £720m. Globally, McDonald's sales reached over US $25 bn. The average UK customer spends £2.99 per visit to McDonald's.

⊗ In 1994, McDonald's UK customers consumed 42,000 tonnes of French fries, 5.5m gallons of milk and 335m hamburger buns.

⊗ The world's busiest McDonald's is on Red Square in Moscow, serving as many as 50,000 people each day.

⊗ Since 1955, when McDonald's first restaurant opened in suburban Chicago, McDonald's has sold over 100 billion hamburgers.

✪ By the end of 1994, more than 60,000 people had received training at McDonald's Hamburger University in East Finchley, London, or at one of two regional training centres.

✪ McDonald's 'Golden Arches' is the second most recognised brand in the world. McDonald's proudly serves the best known brand in the world, Coca-Cola!

Study the McFacts above. Discuss whether you think that McDonald's success has been due to a product-oriented or customer-oriented approach towards marketing. Also, identify what you consider to be its major marketing objectives.

PRODUCT, PRICE, PLACE AND PROMOTION

The ingredients of marketing are known as the 'Four Ps'. They involve matching the product to consumer needs, determining the price, deciding where and how the product or service should be placed (distributed) in the market and promoting it through publicity, advertising and sales techniques. The marketing department will develop an appropriate marketing strategy which involves identifying the most important components of the marketing operation, so as to determine the best **marketing mix** of the 'Four Ps' for its target market.

The market has to be targeted because it is unlikely that an organisation can, or wants to, provide a range of products or services with sufficient variation to satisfy all customers. In **targeting,** the organisation should conduct detailed market research into the characteristics of its potential customers including their socio-economic class, age, household type, gender, personal values and geographical location. This information will allow the organisation to divide the market into groups or **segments**. The organisation should target the segment of the market that offers the best prospects for it to achieve its objectives. By targeting in this way, it is possible for the organisation to develop a marketing mix which satisfies the needs of a clearly defined set of customers.

PRODUCT

When designing a strategy for a product, it is important to identify precisely what is being purchased in terms of benefits and how these help to satisfy a particular need. This means that it is essential to be clear as to exactly what the product provides. For example, Theodore Levitt, a leading figure in marketing in the USA in the 1960s, identified the fact that nobody buys drills: they buy the ability to make holes, which means that if a more efficient and cost-effective way of making holes became available people would turn to it. In fact, a product or service may provide satisfaction at three levels (see *Fig 3.3*).

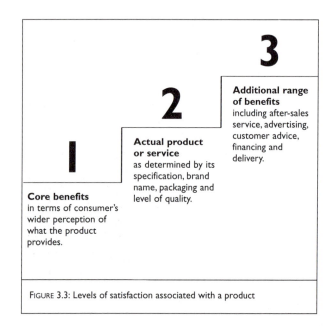

FIGURE 3.3: Levels of satisfaction associated with a product

These levels may be applied to products sold by, for example, the Body Shop. In this case, the **core benefits** might be viewed in terms of buying natural products, which make the consumer feel 'at one' with nature, as they are made from ingredients which do not damage the environment or infringe animal 'rights'. The actual products are created through extensive laboratory research. They are of high quality, are associated with an internationally-known brand name and are sold in a range of sizes with the minimum of packaging. The additional benefits associated with the Body Shop's products are in terms of the advice sheets which are available in the shops, the product knowledge of the staff, the recycling of containers, and the fact that, through purchasing a product, consumers feel that they are supporting a human or animal 'rights' project or action which is beneficial to the environment.

When developing a product, a marketing department must identify the three levels of satisfaction and then design a strategy that allows them to be achieved. This includes consideration of issues concerning branding, packaging, labeling and the development of a range of products to cover all the stages of a product life cycle.

Branding helps to identify a product and differentiate it from those of competitors. It is used to establish consumer loyalty and, in so doing, makes demand more price inelastic. It also can convey a feeling of quality and reliability. For example, the name of Heinz is known by most consumers, who associate it with high-quality food products, especially beans, for which they are probably prepared to pay slightly more.

In certain cases, manufacturers may sell into different segments of the market under a variety of brand names. Unilever sell washing detergents under the names of *Persil, Surf, Radion, Wisk, Lux* and *Stergene*. The ultimate success in branding is when the brand name becomes associated with the brand category, as with Levi's jeans and Kleenex tissues.

Packaging can combine with branding to differentiate the product. It also helps to attract attention, describe the product and, ultimately, make the sale; a more affluent consumer is prepared to pay for the convenience, appearance, dependability and prestige that is communicated through better packaging. This is especially true in the case of expensive cosmetics and confectionery.

Labelling contributes to the perceived quality of the packaging and, ultimately, of the product. This is because it helps to identify the product type and the brand clearly. It might also grade the product, describe its features and provide promotion through suitable graphics; and it can add further value to the product by providing educational information on its usage.

THE PACKAGING PRODIGIES

There's a revolution brewing in the tinned food market and it's going to change the lives, we are told, of the millions of consumers who regularly battle with a can-opener and a tin.

The UK's biggest can producers believe the easy-open-end (EOE) tin is about to win widespread acceptance in food markets here – a feat it has already achieved on the Continent. After more than two decades of development, the latest EOE tins are as sturdy as traditional cans, but sport lids that can be ripped off with a ring-pull.

A changeover will not happen overnight, however. 'It's all about timing,' says Francisco Serrano, marketing manager of the food consumer group of CarnaudMetalbox (CMB), the UK's biggest producer of EOE cans. 'Both manufacturers and retailers are now ready to jump.'

According to Gerry Tipple, business and marketing director of Nacanco subsidiary Pechiney, another major

supplier of EOE cans, 'the first sectors to adapt will be premium products.'

This is a trend experienced in other countries where EOE cans are now well-established. CMB's figures show that EOE penetration in canned food has reached 48 per cent in Italy, 35 per cent in Spain and Portugal and 30 per cent in France.

But some UK manufacturers are already opting for EOE cans as a way of making their brands stand out from the field, even if the advantage is only temporary. 'The use of an EOE can is not something you can withdraw and you certainly can't stop competitors from following suit,' says Tipple.

It's a development that will have far reaching effects on pack design as well as the food inside. The switch to EOE is so fundamental that it is normally part of a relaunch or new product introduction, to make sure that none of its impact is lost.

An EOE can costs more, too – 'perhaps 1p per can extra', according to Tipple – and, in a product re-launch, that expense may have to be written off by the manufacturer. Yet Serrano is convinced that people are willing to pay for more convenient packs: 'It's like buying a Mini – you'd pay more for one with doors, and you wouldn't need a can-opener to get into it.'

And the EOE can is not purely functional. Canners hope the easy-open factor will at last drag tins out of a commodity rut, making the packaging an advantage rather than a problem to be coped with.

Campbell's Grocery Products launched the Cianto range of pasta sauces in October 1992 in CMB's Quantum can, a trademarked design aimed at adding value to the EOE tin's existing convenience benefit. Its vertical flutes take print directly on the can's surface. This year, RHM Foods' J A Sharwood followed suit by repositioning its cook-in sauces with the help of Quantum packs.

'Our research showed that people thought the can looked original, and 72 per cent said it was an improvement on ordinary cans,' says Campbell's marketing manager Andrew Lamb. 'It's obviously easier to use and it adds quality to the product's image.'

Sharwood's is tapping into the growth of premium sauces in what is a fast-growing and highly competitive market. 'We knew the packaging would have to reflect a premium product,' says senior product manager Fergus Rose. The usual route is to opt for jars. 'But why,' he asks, 'should consumers pay up to 40 per cent more for something packed in glass?'

HP Foods' approach is different. It sought a longer-term competitive advantage in the children's pasta market, where its brand is dogged by Heinz, and where sales are won or lost according to which character featured on-pack is currently in vogue.

The range was re-launched in August 1993. 'The new EOE can didn't need specific advertising as its benefits are clearly on show at point-of-sale.' says HP Foods' marketing manager Paul Nevett. 'At the re-launch, the rate of sale improved 25 per cent.'

If the can producers' dreams of a ubiquitous EOE tin are realised, then there is a relatively short time available for the big brands to scoop the value-added benefit of rip-top packs. In petfoods, Mars's Pedigree brand was closely followed into EOE cans by arch-rival Spillers and own-label products.

'It gives us a head start,' sums up Sharwood's Rose. 'But in the end, the can only supports what's inside.'

From: *Marketing,* 20 January 1994

ACTIVITY

CarnaudMetalbox Foodcan

Answer the following questions, referring to the above article.

✪ How might the adoption of an EOE can help food producers to differentiate their products?

✪ How might an EOE can add value to the product?

✪ Why is an EOE can more acceptable in an affluent society?

✪ Which level of satisfaction does the EOE relate to?

✪ Why is it likely that, in time, the views of the senior product manager of Sharwood's will prove to be true?

The life cycle of products must be carefully monitored to allow the organisation to maximise its sales and profits as well as produce the optimum amount of the product. Generally, the **product life cycle** takes the form shown in *Fig 3.4.*

An organisation's marketing strategy should reflect the product life cycle and the stage which a particular product has reached. Typically, the following actions will be necessary.

✪ **Development requires heavy expenditure on market research and product development.**

✪ **When a product is introduced, producers should accept that it will take time to become established and, in consequence, promotional expenses will be high.**

✪ **To sustain growth the organisation may increase the quality of the product and add new features or models. Promotional activities will be focused on building consumer commitment and loyalty.**

✪ **Most products are at the stage of maturity which, in some cases, may be extended by moving into other market segments or repositioning in a larger or faster growing segment. In other cases, the quality, features or style of the product may be modified, or the marketing mix adjusted in terms of price, promotion or place.**

✪ **The organisation should accept when the product has gone into decline and be prepared to drop it, attempt to reposition it, or wait for the competition to 'go under', and then pick up the rest of the market.**

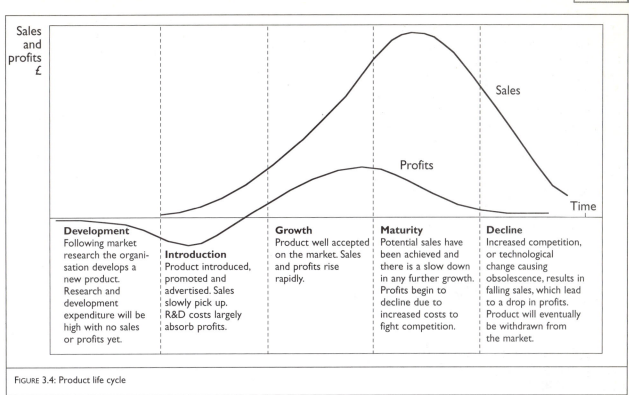

FIGURE 3.4: Product life cycle

Development
Following market research the organisation develops a new product. Research and development expenditure will be high with no sales or profits yet.

Introduction
Product introduced, promoted and advertised. Sales slowly pick up. R&D costs largely absorb profits.

Growth
Product well accepted on the market. Sales and profits rise rapidly.

Maturity
Potential sales have been achieved and there is a slow down in any further growth. Profits begin to decline due to increased costs to fight competition.

Decline
Increased competition, or technological change causing obsolescence, results in falling sales, which lead to a drop in profits. Product will eventually be withdrawn from the market.

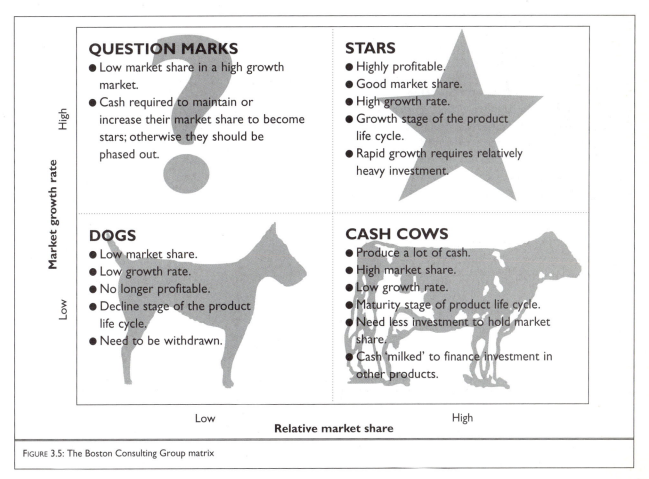

QUESTION MARKS
- Low market share in a high growth market.
- Cash required to maintain or increase their market share to become stars; otherwise they should be phased out.

STARS
- Highly profitable.
- Good market share.
- High growth rate.
- Growth stage of the product life cycle.
- Rapid growth requires relatively heavy investment.

DOGS
- Low market share.
- Low growth rate.
- No longer profitable.
- Decline stage of the product life cycle.
- Need to be withdrawn.

CASH COWS
- Produce a lot of cash.
- High market share.
- Low growth rate.
- Maturity stage of product life cycle.
- Need less investment to hold market share.
- Cash 'milked' to finance investment in other products.

FIGURE 3.5: The Boston Consulting Group matrix

The Boston Consulting Group developed a growth share matrix, which can be combined with the product life cycle to enable an organisation to represent its range of products in terms of market share and growth (see *Fig 3.5*).

Ultimately, an organisation should try to establish a balanced portfolio of products at different stages of development and different positions within the Boston matrix. This should allow for the revenue from one product to help with the development of another, thus ensuring the future survival of the business.

PRICE

Pricing is the only aspect of the marketing mix that directly produces revenue; the other aspects all involve costs. Therefore, it is extremely important to get the pricing strategy right as this will determine the financial success of a particular product and, in so doing, will contribute to the long-term viability of the organisation. The marketing department should set the price in the context of the total marketing mix. If price is not a particularly significant factor for consumers in the target market, strategies relating to quality, promotion and distribution will strongly influence price. If, within the target market, consumers are very price-sensitive, price will strongly influence the other factors making up the marketing mix.

In developing a pricing policy an organisation will have to make plans at several stages.

1   It has to decide its **pricing objectives**, which will reflect the organisation's overall objectives. If its overall objective is to maximise current profits, it will estimate the potential demand and costs and select a price which maximises current profits. But, if it is more interested in achieving security, it may do this by trying to achieve a larger market share, thus setting a lower price. Again, if it is concerned ultimately with status and prestige, it may attempt to create a product of the highest possible quality and, thereby, set the price at a higher level in order to cover the necessary research and development costs.

2   Through market research, the organisation needs to establish the level of demand for the product at different prices. From this it may be possible to derive a demand schedule and determine the degree of **price elasticity**. The more inelastic the demand for the product, the higher the company can set its price.

3   The organisation needs to identify and state clearly the costs associated with the project. Ultimately, the price that is set must, in the long term, recover the costs of producing, distributing and selling the product, plus a profit. The total costs associated with a particular product or service are made up of fixed and variable elements. **Fixed costs** are what has to be paid regardless of output, for example those associated with plant, machinery, rent and rates. **Variable costs** vary directly with the level of output; for example, if output increases, the variable costs associated with inputs such as labour, raw materials and energy will also increase. In formulating a pricing policy, it is necessary to study the behaviour of such costs in the short, long and very long run.

4   Pricing should be competitive, therefore it is important to analyse competitors' prices and offers. Information can be gathered directly, by sending out researchers to compare prices and offers in the shops, or by studying the price lists of competitors.

5   The organisation can now select a pricing method. It must produce a price which reflects the organisation's objectives, the price elasticity of demand for the product, the organisation's costs, and competitors' prices. There are four main approaches to pricing.

Cost-plus pricing is a crude method of pricing. It involves establishing the total costs of producing a particular product, adding a standard margin or 'mark-up' and pricing the product accordingly. For example, if it costs a manufacturer of electrical goods £12 to produce an electric kettle, it could simply add 33.3 per cent as a 'mark-up' and sell the kettle to a retailer for £16. This is a method widely used by many construction companies. In some areas a standard mark-up exists, as in the case of books sold by retailers, which normally have a 33.3 per cent mark-up. The major weakness of this system is that it fails to reflect market forces. If the price has been set too high, the level of sales will suffer; whereas, if it has been set too low, profits may be sacrificed. The system works reasonably well if all the firms within a particular industry broadly use the same methods, so that prices move together.

Target profit pricing involves using break-even analysis (see *Fig 3.6*), which illustrates total costs and total revenues at different volumes of sales. The price must be set at a level at which the firm at least covers its variable costs, otherwise there is no point in continuing production. Profits will occur only at a volume of sales above the break-even level, because only then have fixed and variable costs been covered.

In the case of the example in *Fig 3.6*, at a price of £15 per unit and with the given cost structure, the firm will break even at a volume of 600,000 sales. If the firm's objective is to achieve a target profit of £2m, it would have

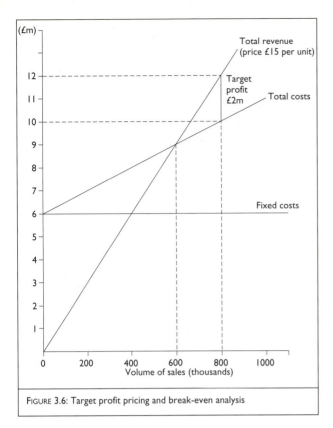

FIGURE 3.6: Target profit pricing and break-even analysis

consumer's perception of the value of a product may, in fact, be lowered if the organisation reduces its price. This is because the consumer may consider a lower price to indicate low quality. Such an attitude is often taken towards electrical goods, where the consumer may feel that, if the product is priced below the expected range, there must be something wrong with it technically, or there must be a poor after-sales service. This view is further supported by the fact that, while some products, such as Heinz baked beans, are more expensive than other brands, consumers are prepared to pay a higher price because they think the product is of a higher quality.

Market rate pricing is often used by smaller organisations which lack the sophisticated research techniques to determine their own prices. Under these circumstances, the solution is simply to charge what is considered to be the going market rate among the organisation's competitors. The price then at least reflects the collective wisdom of the industry.

PLACE

The marketing department has to 'deliver' the product to the consumer as and when it is required. The extent to which this is achieved depends upon decisions regarding the **location** of the production or service organisation, the availability of the product or service and the method by which it is distributed.

Locational decisions should take account of the convenience of access for customers. The development of shopping precincts and out-of-town shopping centres and hypermarkets means that many consumers expect to be able to buy a range of products from one point. This is time-saving for the consumers, who can obtain all their needs 'in one go'.

The logical development of this is that certain types of businesses, which provide complementary products or services, will seek to be located close to each other. For example, estate agents, building societies and solicitors may prefer to be in close proximity to provide a comprehensive service in the buying and selling of houses. Similarly, fast food outlets, pubs, clubs and cinemas may combine to create an area for entertainment, or a component supplier may decide to locate its operations nearby a manufacturing organisation on a business park.

There are circumstances where customer convenience may have to take second place to other locational factors. Typically, this is when cost factors have a more significant effect than price in the marketing mix. These costs could include those of transport of the finished product, or relate to the need for special site facilities, such as storage space or a means of disposing of waste matter, or the availability of a suitable supply of skilled labour (and, thus, the wages

to achieve a level of sales of 800,000 at a price of £15 per unit. It is possible that by charging a higher price the firm may achieve its objective of £2m profit with a lower volume of sales. This is because the slope of the total revenue curve would be steeper, so the firm would break even at a lower volume of sales. Ultimately, the price and volume of sales at which the firm will achieve this target level of profit will depend on its demand schedule and the price elasticity of demand. Therefore, this break-even analysis is of value only if it is viewed in the context of the demand situation facing the firm.

Perceived value pricing relates to the non-price variables in the marketing mix, which help to raise the consumers' perception of the product and, in so doing, their willingness to pay a higher price. Take, as an example, a simple product like fish and chips. If it was served in newspaper at a fish bar a consumer might be prepared to pay £1.75 for it. On the other hand, if the consumer ate it as a meal in a cafe a price of £3.50 might be considered acceptable. In the atmosphere of a restaurant the same meal might appear on the menu at £6.50, and in a hotel restaurant a resident might pay £8 for the same dish as a course of an evening meal. The higher price can be charged due to the difference in the surroundings and atmosphere in which the fish and chips are eaten.

This method of pricing relies upon accurate research into how people view a particular product and give value to the non-price variables in the marketing mix. The that have to be paid). To take an example, the locational decision of a single-site chemical plant is likely to be largely determined by requirements for a particular type of site and the availability of suitable employees.

Organisations seek to make decisions regarding place which ensure the **availability** of products or services when customers need them and in the quantity they require. This means that the organisation of production, storage and distribution must contribute towards the realisation of the consumer's expectations. For example, consumers who buy a particular make of car need to be confident that, if they visit the spares department of the main dealer, the component or part they require is available immediately or can be easily obtained. This is only possible if there has been an attempt to balance the production, distribution and stocking of spares in relation to the number of complete finished vehicles which have been sold.

The channels and system of distribution determine the way in which products reach the market. The marketing department seeks to establish the most efficient system so that the product is available at the right time and in the right place. A successful system depends upon the efficiency and speed of transportation, the quality of packaging, the efficiency of the stock control and storage system and the sophistication of the ordering system.

The effectiveness of the **distribution** system also depends upon the channels the product may go through. Traditionally, manufacturers have sold products to wholesalers in large quantities which are then sold to retailers in smaller, more manageable quantities. The benefits of this system have been that it allows the wholesaler to handle large shipments from the manufacturer and provide the storage for, and transportation of, the product to the retailer. In recent years, a number of manufacturers have decided to by-pass the wholesaler and deal directly with retailers or consumers. This enables savings to be made and provides a quicker response to market trends. Boots and Laura Ashley have taken this a stage further by having a vertically integrated operation, from manufacture to retailing.

PROMOTION

The purpose of promotion is to communicate directly with potential or existing customers, to encourage them to purchase the product or service and recommend it to others. The main promotional tools are sales promotions, public relations and advertising. Essentially, any promotional activity concentrates on the distinctive features of a product, which are known as its unique selling points.

In designing a promotional activity the marketing department has to take several steps.

- ✪ **Identifying and targeting the required market segment.**

- ✪ **Establishing the purpose of the promotion in the context of the buying process; that is, recognition of need, consideration and evaluation of how to satisfy that need, making a choice, and evaluating the choice which may result in a repeat purchase. This will determine whether the promotion seeks to increase potential or existing customers' awareness or knowledge of the product, or to strengthen their preference for it or their determination to purchase it.**

- ✪ **Taking decisions on a suitable promotional message for the target audience. In some cases it may be appropriate to appeal to the consumers' emotions, in others to their reason.**

- ✪ **Selecting a suitable form of media for the target audience.**

- ✪ **Evaluating the promotional activity by measuring feedback in terms of who becomes aware of the product, uses it, and expresses satisfaction with it.**

The choice of promotional activity will ultimately be determined by what the organisation can afford to spend, the type of product and market, and the stage reached by the product in its life cycle.

Sales promotions may be directed at the consumer or the trade. Consumer promotions are used to encourage potential consumers to try a product and, hopefully, to purchase it again. This may be attempted through such methods as giving free samples, gifts, vouchers and cash refunds. Trade promotions are aimed at distributors to encourage them to stock a particular product. This may be attempted through such methods as cash incentives and the payment of bonuses.

Public relations is an area used to promote a positive image of a company's achievements. It involves gaining favourable publicity and developing a perception that the company is socially responsible. It also helps to build awareness of the organisation and develop a preference for its products. It may be aimed not only at potential and existing consumers but also the organisation's suppliers and distributors and, where appropriate, any government departments or pressure groups which might be interested in its activities. Major retailers, like Marks and Spencer, Sainsbury's and Tesco, spend a great deal on public relations, to promote a responsible, caring and high-quality image. The major public relations tools involve the use of publicity, publications such as newsletters and brochures, corporate image and sponsorship.

Advertising involves the use of the media by an organisation to inform, persuade and remind potential and existing consumers about its products and activities. It may also be used to encourage customers into a particular retail outlet. In deciding on an appropriate method of, or medium for, advertising an organisation will take several steps:

- ☺ **deciding on the purpose of the advertisement: whether it is concerned essentially with imparting information, persuading new consumers or reminding existing ones;**

- ☺ **fixing the budget for the advertising campaign in the context of sales and the amount spent by competitors;**

- ☺ **identifying, designing and evaluating the required message (often carried out by an advertising agency);**

- ☺ **deciding on the medium or media, including newspapers, magazines, television, cinema, radio, hoardings, catalogues, circulars and leaflets (also often carried out by an agency); and**

- ☺ **evaluating the effectiveness of the advertisement in terms of communications and sales.**

It is possible to measure the probable value of advertising expenditure by calculating the elasticity of advertising (EA). This is done by dividing the proportionate change in sales volume by the proportionate change in advertising expenditure. If EA is greater than one, increasing advertising expenditure is probably worthwhile, as it will create a more than proportionate increase in sales volume.

PENGUIN TARGETS KIDS

McVitie's is turning to character licensing for the first time on its Penguin brand in a bid to strengthen its dominance of the children's countline market.

It is jumping on the Captain Scarlet bandwagon and testing out a new size multi-pack – 12 Penguin biscuits priced at 99p – from the end of this month. The pack will feature details of a Captain Scarlet promotion, offering a torch in return for proofs of purchase.

Penguin marketing manager Chris Pass admitted the decision to license an outside character instead of relying solely on Penguin's own figurehead – which itself has been licensed out to third parties in the past – is a 'potentially dangerous' move.

'It is something we have been very cognisant of in preparing the TV advertising,' he said, referring to creative work from Publicis that breaks on February 26. It continues the recent theme of using footage of live penguins, but this time in the form of a Captain Scarlett spoof.

The 1960s character was chosen, according to Pass, because 'the character is popular and topical and we are attempting to build playground credibility'.

Penguin, which McVitie's describes as the biggest selling children's countline brand with £43m sales, has an opportunity to build sales, claimed Pass. While confectionery brands are increasingly frowned upon by more health-conscious parents and school teachers, Penguin 'has a biscuit heritage and is considered much more acceptable. We've experienced a big plus.'

The new-size pack compares with the 63p seven-pack and the £1.25 14-pack. The promotion will be monitored 'very carefully' and may result in a permanent 99p pack of 12.

From: *Marketing*, 17 February 1994

ACTIVITY

Answer the following questions, referring to the above article.

- ☺ **What stage do you think that the Penguin chocolate biscuit has reached in its product life cycle?**

- ☺ **Where would 'the Penguin' be positioned in terms of the Boston Matrix?**

- ☺ **Does the creation of the new 12-pack for 99p suggest that McVitie's considers the demand for Penguins to be price elastic?**

- ✪ **Analyse the reasons for the sustained success of the Penguin brand.**

- ✪ **Identify the market segment that McVitie's is targeting with its Captain Scarlet promotion, and the major objective behind the promotion.**

PORTFOLIO ASSIGNMENT

HI-TEC MARKETING

Read the following **HI-TEC** case study.

TASK
You are employed as a marketing assistant for the family firm of Marshall's, which is a specialist producer of top of the range walking and golf shoes.

Jane Marshall, the oldest child of the founder of the business has recently taken over as managing director. She wishes to bring the company into the modern world by repositioning it in the market and diversifying into a wider range of sports goods. In preparation for designing a strategy to achieve this objective she asks you to examine the marketing activities of **HI-TEC**.

Using the information in the panel (below), produce a report which analyses **HI-TEC's** marketing strategy and the reasons for its success. Consider whether such an approach to marketing could be adopted by Marshall's. No futher information or assistance in carrying out this assignment should be sought (or is needed) from **HI-TEC** Sports.

THE DEVELOPMENT OF A BRAND

HI-TEC Sports plc was founded in 1974 in the appropriately named village of Shoeburyness, Essex. The company's original success came as a result of the design and development of HI-TEC's first ever shoe, specifically designed for the then fast-growing game of squash – the HI-TEC Squash, of which over ten million pairs have been sold worldwide.

The early 1980s, within the worldwide sporting goods industry, saw an important move towards increasingly complex materials and shoe constructions.

With consumers starting to become increasing discerning, a product's features had to compete effectively to be considered among the most advanced in its field. With this in mind, the HI-TEC name and logo were created and launched in 1982. The brand reflects the following:

- ✪ **a stated commitment to offer all consumers advanced sports footwear which provides performance, top quality and guaranteed comfort;**

- ✪ **technologically advanced research;**

- ✪ **detailed design carried out with the help of computer technology; and**

✪ **development of increasingly complex manufacturing.**

When reproduced in print, the HI-TEC brand name is always accompanied underneath by the HI-TEC 'harpoon' or 'sideflash', as it is sometimes known. The 'harpoon' is key to HI-TEC's global brand strategy since it is the single most important means of hallmarking and identifying a HI-TEC shoe, textile garment or accessory, whether appearing alone on the outer side of a show, for example, or accompanied in an embroidered format by the HI-TEC name.

The corporate colours of the HI-TEC name and logo are the same worldwide – blue and red. These colours were chosen specifically for their association with both the British and American flags: HI-TEC's two most important markets are the UK and the USA.

THE UK OPERATION

In the United Kingdom, the commercial strategy has always been to concentrate on the mid-price ranges with a wide customer base including both sports and shoe shops. This policy has meant that HI-TEC has, for the last three years, been among the top three brands in the UK market. It supplies over 4,500 retail accounts, approximately 45 per cent of which are sports retailers. Major accounts include Olympus (part of Sears), Champion (part of the Burton Group), Intersport and the British Shoe Corporation.

Sports retailers are a vital link between HI-TEC and the end consumer. They have the responsibility of helping consumers to choose the right shoe, balanced with their own need to build a profitable business.

INTERNATIONAL EXPANSION

HI-TEC is taking a planned approach to international expansion. HI-TEC believes that the sporting goods industry is increasingly global in nature with the needs of consumers increasingly homogenous. It is for this reason that competition is no longer limited to the domestic market, and the company is therefore building a worldwide brand.

HI-TEC shoe, textile and accessory collections are currently marketed in over 70 countries worldwide. Strategic markets outside the UK have been identified and subsidiary companies established. The USA and Canada, Europe (in particular Ireland) and South Africa all play a key role in HI-TEC's international expansion plans. Its American organisation is the fastest growing of all group companies, now among the 'top 20' footwear brands in the USA, with its market leading range of lightweight rugged outdoor footwear. Elsewhere, in continental Europe HI-TEC has adapted its operations to the creation of a single European market with distributor companies in the Benelux countries, Germany, France and Spain. With the free movement of goods now permitted, all European Union countries are serviced with stocks held in a central European warehouse, in the Netherlands.

All international operations are subject to central control over product collections and quality as well as commercial policy and customer service operations. A basic central marketing directive exists but HI-TEC recognises that strong cultural and language differences still prevail, so country-specificactivities are carefully monitored to local conditions and needs.

THE CREATION AND MARKETING OF HI-TEC's PRODUCT COLLECTIONS

This starts with the continual feedback from HI-TEC's worldwide subsidiaries and distributors of ever-changing market information and trends, changing consumer attitudes and evolving design ideas and new sports. This data is interpreted into a twice-yearly design brief which forms the basis of the new collection.

The new collection is then presented to the sports and shoe trade by means of bulk sampling of the entire HI-TEC sales organisation, both in the UK and worldwide. During HI-TEC's selling period, it also exhibits at a number of international trade venues to assist in determining demand.

Orders are then placed with factories located all over the world, most notably in Indonesia, Korea, The Philippines, China and Vietnam. The company recognises the importance of top quality and delivery reliability which is why the production process (factory orders, quality control, scheduling and shipping) is managed by its own Far Eastern offices in Hong Kong, Korea, Taiwan, Indonesia and The Philippines. The finished product is then shipped by sea in containers to one of HI-TEC's warehouses and then sold to its customers worldwide.

Each country then operates a marketing campaign to support the products that have been developed. A typical campaign will normally concentrate on the following broad mix, adapted to local market conditions. Other elements may, of course, be added where relevant.

1 A product range constructed to meet key price points and cosmetic criteria; for example, Mediterranean countries traditionally require more brightly coloured products.

2 A distribution network capitalising on traditional sports and shoe retail outlets as well as opportunities to supply sports clubs.

3 A trade promotion campaign in which HI-TEC Sports UK invites key sports and shoe trade buyers to exhibitions and stockroom events; co-ordinates quarterly mailshots to all accounts, with brochures and informing them of company news, personnel updates, new collections, pricing issues and special offers; advertises in trade magazines and ensures 'mentions' in articles on general new product collections; and ensures the salesforce regularly

presents an exciting product and explains the benefits to be gained from working with HI-TEC.

4 A consumer promotion campaign in which HI-TEC Sports UK engages the following: Ian Woosnam (golf), Henri Leconte (tennis), Roy Keane, Paul Merson, Denis Wise and over 50 other Premier League players (soccer) and Jansher Khan, the world's number one squash player, and four of the world's 'top 10' lady squash players. Also, event sponsorship, including the British Open Squash Tournament, stands at all major golf events in the UK, and stands at walking and hiking events; official associations, including as official supplier to the Wimbledon Championships, the Professional Golf Associations of Europe and the International Squash Players' Association; and a print campaign in specialist magazines.

PORTFOLIO ASSIGNMENT

INVITING SPEAKERS

As a school or college group, contact a marketing or public relations representative from a local company and a voluntary organisation or charity. In each case ask the organisation to send copies of its annual report and accounts as well as any in-house literature relating to its marketing strategy.

Invite the representatives to your school (or college) to make a short presentation on how their organisation reconciles the need to be oriented towards customers or members with its overall strategic business and financial objectives. Ask them to supply examples of how their organisation has developed through:

✪ the development of existing or new markets;

✪ the maintenance and increase of market share;

✪ innovation and the development of new products;

✪ the modification and relaunching of old products or the achievement of technological breakthroughs.

On the basis of the information supplied by the organisations prepare questions regarding the possible conflict between customer orientation, productivity and profitability; the use of market research; and the composition of the marketing mix.

Make notes individually during the presentations and prepare questions on the major points and issues covered.

Adopting the role of a business journalist, use your notes as the basis for an article entitled 'Putting the Consumer First in both the Business and Voluntary Sectors'.

Marketing research and product development

THE VALUE OF RESEARCH

Marketing research provides information that helps organisations to recognise and respond to market opportunities and to develop suitable products to meet market needs. It enables organisations to find out which goods and services people want, the price they are prepared to pay, where they prefer to buy the product, and how products should be promoted.

Ultimately, by carrying out marketing research, the organisation can identify key factors which relate to customer satisfaction at three levels. These are: the essential (or 'core') benefits associated with a product, i.e. what the customer seeks to obtain by buying it; the product specification, including branding, packaging and quality; and additional benefits associated with after-sales service, advertising, customer advice, financing and delivery.

All these factors add value to the product, thus increasing its competitiveness and potential returns. For example, obtaining suitable information regarding the entertainment needs of young people contributed to the dominance of Sega and Nintendo in the computer games market. Similarly, it helped Horn Abbot achieve international success with *Trivial Pursuit*.

AREAS OF RESEARCH

Marketing research information is either **quantitative** or **qualitative**. The former is essentially numerical (how many people buy a product, how often they buy it), whereas qualitative data relate to consumer attitudes.

In order to make sound marketing decisions, organisations need to collect and analyse research information in six main areas.

PRODUCT RESEARCH

This includes both the development of new products and the improvement of existing ones. Before any changes are made, products will be put through a series of tests to

ACTIVITY

Make a list of five products which have been particularly successful in meeting a market need, and suggest how marketing research may have helped to identify that need.

investigate features such as design, materials or ingredients, colour durability, ease of handling, fitness for purpose, and operating capacity.

One of the problems in developing a new product is that customers are obviously unfamiliar with it, so their reaction, when shown a prototype or told about it, may be misleading. This is likely to be especially true where the product breaks entirely new ground, for example in terms of technology. Initially, customers may resist the unfamiliar, but when the benefits are recognised the innovation may be quickly adopted. When the 'hole in the wall' cash dispenser was introduced, customers were wary of dealing with a machine. They felt it lacked the reassurance of a human transaction. However, the 24-hour access provided by automatic tellers was soon seen as such a significant benefit that their use grew rapidly.

The importance of psychology is widely recognised in product research. This is because consumers can be motivated in their purchases by the status or prestige which they believe, and maybe know from their friends, that ownership of a particular product confers. Brand labelling can play an important part in image making.

Market tests are carried out to reach decisions as to how products should be packaged, both in terms of the type of container used (where applicable) and its overall appearance. Important factors include the materials used, the design, labelling, robustness, weight and ease of storage. Tests for comparative purposes may be carried out on competitors' products to help pinpoint advantages or deficiencies in the new or improved product.

Testing of the product and its packaging may indicate features which are superfluous and might be 'dropped', facilitating greater standardisation in production. The organisation may also be concerned to ensure that it has a sufficient range of output to allow it to compete in all areas of the market that may prove profitable. After-sales service records may indicate areas for improvement or means of raising the quality of the service provided.

In the 1990s, market research has increasingly been applied in new product development, as the article excerpt in the panel below shows.

RESEARCH PROPELS INNOVATION

Innovate or die. This is the daunting challenge facing companies and it's easier said than done, given the high failure of new products introduced into the marketplace.

Market research is increasingly being used to reduce those failures and save money. Answers are needed at a number of steps in the new product development cycle and research can provide the necessary guidance.

But market research has not always been regarded as a guiding light. According to Julian Bond, NPD [new product development] managing director at Research International: 'Market research used to be a very minor part of decision-making in the '80s and was used to back up decisions that were already made.' Bond says most manufacturers' historic use of market researchers was like a drunk's need of a lamp post. 'It was used more for support than illumination,' he says.

Those days are long gone. Manufacturers are now looking to research to point out how to fine-tune new products as well as predict new buyer volumes. They are listening ever more closely to their customers.

The first question a manufacturer must ask is whether or not it is reading the marketplace correctly. In other words, are new product ideas on the right track with consumers? Market research can shed light on what consumers like and don't like about a product innovation idea. This feedback can then be incorporated into the new product design to ensure it is what consumers want.

Such early testing can also be useful for helping a manufacturer choose between several alternative NPD ideas. The idea which has the most likely chance of succeeding with consumers can become a prototype.

From *Marketing*, January 27 1994

RESEARCH INTO DISTRIBUTION

This helps to determine how consumers would prefer new or existing products to be made available.

Marketing research information may be gathered to

ACTIVITY

Think of four products that consumers might think of as being of particularly high status, and explain why this should be the case.

---

measure the effectiveness of the sales force in terms of the cost of calls and the number and size of orders. Also, different methods of distribution, such as mail order, using a wholesaler, or direct selling can be investigated, as may the performance of individual distribution outlets. This information will help to ensure that strong distribution areas can be built upon, while unprofitable products and sales in unrewarding areas can be discontinued. Contact with those purchasing on behalf of distributive outlets or trades will provide useful opinions on the organisation's marketing techniques, when compared with those of competitors.

Sales staff will generally operate under some form of incentive scheme. New schemes may result in increased effort on the part of those seeking orders from customers or distributors. Research can be carried out to determine the most effective incentive scheme.

RESEARCH INTO PROMOTION

This helps to determine how effective various promotional and advertising activities are in persuading consumers to want a particular product. The impact of advertisements, brochures, exhibitions, sales demonstrations and media publicity can be assessed; for example, in terms of the number of resulting enquiries and sales.

SOCIAL AND OTHER TRENDS

The way businesses operate is obviously influenced by the wider political, economic, social and technological environment. These are referred to by an acronym as **PEST factors**. By analysing trends and developments, organisations can spot new market opportunities and threats.

POLITICAL FACTORS

The actions of government have a major effect on business and markets, including creating (or dampening) demand for particular products or for consumer items in general. This is achieved by setting public spending levels, allocating funds for special programmes (such as to buy computers for schools), changes in taxation and interest rates for borrowers, and the introduction of new (or the abolition of existing) laws, regulations and licence arrangements.

Increasingly, in a global economy, such decisions are reached internationally, through the European Union, the biannual 'economic summit' of the heads of the seven largest economies and the work of organisations such as GATT (the General Agreement on Tariffs and Trade). For example, changes in the European Common Agricultural Policy have directly influenced opportunities for milk production by dairy farmers.

The case study (see panel) shows how one organisation has gained a market advantage from both UK and European changes.

SIGNS AND LABELS

The success of Signs and Labels Ltd shows that new laws can mean business. Formed in 1970, the company's successful identification and exploitation of market opportunities arising from Government regulations resulted in two decades of steady growth. Throughout that time, Government-introduced regulations required companies to be more thorough in labelling and signing dangers. The Safety Signs regulations of 1980 sparked huge growth in the UK market, which was recently further stimulated by Control of Substances Hazardous to Health rules. A member of the British Standards Institute (BSI), the company monitors safety developments through BSI publications and safety journals. Since safety signs are based on common [European Union] standards, Signs and Labels sees growth opportunities in the European market and has opened an office in Germany.

From *Marketing: the way forward*, Department of Trade and Industry, 1992

ECONOMIC FACTORS

The United Kingdom's economic performance determines its level of **national income**. How this is distributed, together with the distribution of wealth, ultimately determines the standard of living enjoyed by individual members of society. This, in turn, influences consumer spending and, thereby, market opportunities.

A standard measure of a country's economic performance is gross domestic product (GDP). This is the total value of goods and services produced, usually expressed annually and *per capita*, i.e. the total divided by the population of the country. GDP is a useful broad indicator both of the size of a national market and of comparative living standards in different countries.

However, while adjustment is made for the varying price levels in different countries in calculating GDP, the figures do not show the extent to which spending power is widely spread or concentrated in relatively few hands. Nor do they take into account levels of taxation, which can substantially reduce consumer spending power.

The trend in the UK has been for GDP to increase steadily decade by decade. Total wealth created in the early 1990s was about double that of the early 1960s. However, compared to our major economic competitors (in Europe, North America and the Pacific Rim), economic growth has been modest, and the UK has been slipping down the international league table. Nevertheless, while the UK was ranked eighteenth among the 24 leading industrial nations in terms of GDP *per capita* in 1990, once Britain's relatively low taxation was taken into account, we were ranked sixth in terms of consumer spending.

The size of various national economies, their productiveness (the amount of wealth created divided by the number of people living in the country), and how much is left on average for personal spending after taxation are shown in *Fig 3.7*. For example, Greece's economy is twice as big as Ireland's, but the Irish economy is 45 per cent more productive and, after taxation, the average Greek

	GDP totals (US $ bn.)	GDP per capita	Consumption per capita (US $)
Australia	272.5	15,951	9,458
Belgium	163.5	16,405	10,153
Canada	509.0	19,120	11,289
Denmark	86.2	16,765	8,773
France	983.5	17,431	10,516
Germany	1,156.6	18,291	9,883
Greece	74.5	7,349	5,317
Ireland	37.3	10,659	5,904
Italy	923.6	16,021	9,907
Japan	2,178.5	17,634	10,073
Netherlands	235.7	15,766	9,276
Spain	459.4	11,792	7,360
Sweden	144.4	16,867	8,733
Switzerland	142.7	20,997	11,982
United Kingdom	902.5	15,720	9,948
USA	5,392.2	21,449	14,465

FIGURE 3.7: GDP totals and per capita and private final consumption expenditure 1990, selected countries, in US dollars
Note: Private final consumption expenditure is the total spent by households and non-profit organisations on new goods and services less net sales of second-hand goods.
Source: *National Accounts Vol.1 Main Aggregates 1960-1990*, Organisation for Economic Co-operation and Development, Paris, 1992

or Irish person has roughly the same amount to spend. Note the very high levels of taxation in some countries, such as Sweden and Denmark, and the huge size of the American market. *Fig 3.8* gives the GDP totals and *per capita* figures for some less developed countries.

As has already been remarked, the national picture does not tell us about the distribution of spending power among various groups. If you break down the UK population into five groups in terms of their disposable household income, in 1991 the 'top fifth' accounted for slightly more than 40 per cent of overall spending, whereas the 'bottom fifth' accounted for only about six per cent.

	GDP total (US $ bn.)	GDP per capita (US $)
Algeria	45	1,698
Brazil	358	2,300
Ghana	6	400
Iran	90	1,500
Israel	55	12,000
Jamaica	4	1,400
Nigeria	30	250
Singapore	38	13,900
South Africa	104	2,600
South Korea	270	6,253

FIGURE 3.8: GDP totals and *per capita* for selected less developed countries 1992, in US dollars

The disparity between rich and poor becomes even more marked when wealth (income and assets) is considered. In 1991, just one per cent of the population accounted for 18 per cent of 'marketable wealth' in the UK and the 10 per cent most rich accounted for half. Moreover, if you remove the value of housing (by far and away the biggest asset for most people), the disparities become even greater, with the five per cent most rich owning half of the wealth.

Differences in **wealth distribution** obviously have implications for marketing, with greater opportunities amongst the top 20 per cent of households for the sale of luxury items such as large houses, lavish furnishings, fast cars, expensive boats and exotic holidays. On the other hand, amongst the poorest 20 per cent a market opportunity exists for basic items including food, clothing and household goods. This may be reflected in the number of discount shops and street traders in poorer areas.

Changes in the composition of the assets included as personal wealth may result in market opportunities as individuals switch between property, shares and financial assets. Such changes may be brought about through inheritance.

Ultimately, changes in income and wealth normally affect overall expenditure. *Fig 3.9* gives a detailed breakdown of **household expenditure** at constant (1990) prices, which removes the inflation element and makes comparisons possible. Total household expenditure increased by 66 per cent in real terms between 1971 and 1992, which was in line with the overall increase in national income during the period.

ACTIVITY

Using data in *Fig 3.9* draw a graph plotting the changes in household spending for various consumer items in the period 1971 to 1992.

Calculate percentage changes in spending for different items between 1971 and 1992, and suggest reasons for these changes in spending.

	1971	1981	1986	1990	1992
Food	87	91	95	100	101
Alcohol	72	91	96	100	95
Tobacco	138	122	102	100	93
Clothing/Footwear	52	67	92	100	99
Fuel/Power	86	94	102	100	106
Household durables	53	69	86	100	100
Buying vehicles	51	59	81	100	77
Running vehicles	47	65	84	100	97
TV/Video	19	46	77	100	101
Books/Newspapers	101	97	92	100	96
Meals/Catering	55	58	72	100	92

FIGURE 3.9: Household expenditure 1971–1992, selected items, at constant (1990) prices
Note: Household durables cover items such as washing machines, refrigerators and microwave ovens.
Source: *Social Trends 1994*, CSO

Compare the results and draw up a league table ranking the rates of change.

Draw conclusions about the extent to which the rankings have been influenced by changes in the distribution of income and wealth and consider the implications for market opportunities.

SOCIAL FACTORS

These largely involve **demographic changes** which cover age, ethnicity and other characteristics. It is important for marketing because it reveals trends which influence demand for particular types of products. Take age, for example. The UK has an ageing population. This is because people are living longer and, compared to the 'boom' years from the late-1940s into the early-1960s, couples are having fewer babies. By the year 2021, nearly one in five of the population will be aged over 65, compared to only one in 10 in 1951. One in 27 people (and one in 20 women) are now aged 80 or older. Conversely, under-16s today comprise only one in five of the population compared to one in four in the 1960s. It is not surprising, therefore, that while the late-1950s and 1960s saw the rapid growth of 'youth culture', with new entertainment and clothing products, in recent times there has been a growing 'grey market'. A good example is the success of Saga Holidays, which caters specifically for the retired. Meanwhile, the 'baby boomers' have become middle-aged, creating a lucrative market for restauranteurs, travel companies and those selling financial services, such as insurance and pension plans.

ACTIVITY

Make a list of products for which demand is likely to increase due to the move, in the next two decades, of the baby boom generation into retirement. Clues can be found by looking at the growing current 'grey market'.

However, overall population trends can disguise what is happening with particular groups. For example, some ethnic minority groups have very young populations. Over four in 10 of those from the Pakistani and Bangladeshi communities are aged under 16. Among the Afro-Caribbean population there is a disproportionate number of 16-29 year-olds (30 per cent of the total compared to only 21 per cent among whites). This reflects the wave of immigration from the Caribbean in the 1950s, with couples starting families in the 1960s and 1970s.

Market evidence of the purchasing power of young black people can be seen in sales of sportswear and leisure products, but also in mobile phones and demand for college places and educational products (a higher proportion of black young people go to college than do whites). About one in 10 of the UK population now comprises 'people of colour', and this has influenced demand generally, for example in young people's fashions. It has also created important new product areas, such as black hair and beauty products.

SOUL-D ON HEALTHY FOOD!

Black people spend more money on nutritious food and eat better quality diets than White people, according to a recently published survey by the Joseph Rowntree Foundation.

Its report says: 'Black households had more varied and healthier diets and to some extent better mineral and vitamin intakes. Evidence supports the study's findings that Black parents always cooked their food from raw, fresh ingredients, and provided a highly varied diet for their families.'

Ironically, Black families spent slightly less – an average of £40 a week, compared to £42 for a counterpart White family.

Liz Dowler of the Joseph Rowntree Foundation said their survey revealed that Black families put more emphasis on eating well seasoned, quality food. 'It is a traditional thing that has nothing to do with income. Many Black people still cook the traditional way. Good food is a priority.'

From The Voice, 11 July 1995

Movement of the population geographically also has significance for marketing. The counties with the fastest population growth in the 1980s were Cambridgeshire, Buckinghamshire and Cornwall, with Belfast and the Scottish Isles experiencing the biggest decreases. Such changes may create opportunities or pose threats for construction companies, makers of furniture and durable household goods, and service and entertainment providers.

Another indicator is **household size**. This has fallen in the last three decades, with a considerable increase in the proportion of people who live alone (see *Fig 3.10*). The biggest group comprises women aged 60 or older, although in the period 1971 to 2001 the proportion of this group within the population as a whole is not expected to increase greatly. The big increase concerns men of working age (under 65). By the year 2001, one in 10

	1961	1971	1981	1991
1 person	14	18	22	27
2 people	30	32	32	34
3 people	23	19	17	16
4 people	18	17	18	16
5 people	9	8	7	5
6 or more people	7	6	4	2
Number of house– holds (millions)	16.2	18.2	19.5	21.9

FIGURE 3.10: Households, by size per cents and totals (Great Britain)
Source: *Social Trends 1994*, CSO

households is expected to come into this category, compared to fewer than one in 25 at the beginning of the 1970s.

From a marketing point of view, the decline in household size and the associated growth of one person households has led to a number of market opportunities. For example, construction companies have been able to build more flats, maisonettes and sheltered accommodation; furniture retailers have faced an increased demand for smaller items to go into reduced living areas; demand has risen for home security systems, particularly by elderly people living alone; and food producers and retailers have experienced a growing demand for items packaged in smaller units and as individual meals.

Another significant social trend is the decline in the predominance of the traditional family. Between 1961 and 1991, the proportion of all households comprising a married couple with dependent children fell from just over half (52 per cent) to two-fifths. Nevertheless, it still should be recognised that more people live in this type of family unit than in any other. However, the rise in lone parent families has implications for the way products are promoted. Advertisers need to be careful not to give the impression that only traditional families buy their products.

TECHNOLOGY FACTORS

Developments in technology give rise to new products and market opportunities. For example, the application of technology in the home led to the development of the 'white goods' industry, which makes washing machines, refrigerators, dishwashers, etc. This, in turn, led to the creation of materials and services associated with these goods, such as special types of paints, new materials and plastics, and appropriate detergents for use in the machines.

Many companies have research departments specifically to carry out scientific and technical work leading to new products. For example, pharmaceutical companies spend considerable sums on the development of new drugs and medicines.

ACTIVITY

Select a group of 10 household items bought weekly. Visit a supermarket and identify which of the items have been packaged, presented and promoted to meet the needs of both the one-person household and the traditional family.

From a variety of newspapers and magazines find examples of advertisements for the items included in your shopping basket. Identify those that are not household specific in their presentation.

During the period of a week, video tape any advertisements appearing on television which relate to your 10 items. Classify them according to the type of household to which they are targeted.

Prepare a 10 minute presentation on 'Targeting the household of the 1990s' based on your findings. Illustrate the presentation with advertising examples.

Equally, social and market factors may spark the widespread adoption of a particular technology or create a demand for technologically innovative products. Facsimile technology was invented in the middle of the last century, but it was not until the 1980s that business uses emerged that made it attractive.

Ecological problems can arise from the use of new technologies, for example the pollution of the environment and the disturbance of the balance of the natural forces of regeneration. Causes include the over-felling of trees, the intensive use of chemicals in farming and the uncontrolled emission of toxic waste products. Recognition of these threats to the environment has created a marketing opportunity for products which can claim to be 'green' and are sold to customers who are concerned about the environment.

CONSUMER BEHAVIOUR

Business organisations can only successfully divide the market into different groups (or 'segments') and 'position' their product in terms of giving it a distinctive appeal to particular buyers if they understand the wants of actual and potential customers. They, therefore, need to conduct research into consumer behaviour. There are several aspects of this which can be investigated.

CULTURE

Culture refers to the set of beliefs and behaviour patterns to which different groups and individuals adher. The main influences are family, friends, teachers, politicians, religion and the media, including advertising. For example, the typical young person in Britain in the 1990s expects to own a computer and the games that go with it. This is because today's youngsters have been brought up in an age where they have developed the capacity to read and understand computer instructions, and they are surrounded at school by others who are also using computers.

Cultural shifts take place all the time. In recent years, a greater emphasis has been placed by society on health and fitness. Consequently, market opportunities have opened up for health centres and gyms, sports shops are booming and supermarkets are stocking more low calorie and natural foods.

Any nation or group is made up of several sub-cultures, holding beliefs which, in some measure, make them distinctive. Determining this distinctiveness and applying it to marketing is a task of research; but there are dangers.

One is that the characteristic identified as distinctive may not be relevant. Do Catholics eat more sausages than Protestants? Probably not. Another is that the classification is too crude: it fails to recognise important sub-characteristics within the larger group. An obvious example is the grouping that sometimes happens of ethnic minorities, when, in fact, the differences between, say, those of Chinese, Caribbean and Indian descent are much more significant than the fact that they are not white. There is also the risk of stereotyping, which means transferring the perceived characteristics of a group to the individuals who comprise it. Not all Yorkshire people like brass bands, no more than Scots eat haggis! Nevertheless, some cultural differences are deeply rooted, for example muslims do not eat pork; and generalisations can be valid. Cultural factors may also underlie shopping habits (see Fig 3.11)

Sub-cultural groups could also be based on **age.** For example, in 1961 just under 12 per cent of the population was aged 65 or over; by 1991 nearly 16 per cent were in this age group; and this number is projected to rise to just over 22 per cent by 2031. This retired group has its own needs and patterns of consumption. It might be targeted for healthcare products and medical plans, retirement homes, financial packages, particular types of holidays and restaurants, and home security systems.

CLASS

In marketing, the notion of **social class** is used to differentiate groups according to income and occupational status. The Institute of Practitioners in Advertising has identified the following classes, which are very widely applied: higher and intermediate management, administrative or professional (AB); supervisory or clerical, and junior management, administrative or professional (C1); skilled manual workers (C2); and semi-skilled and unskilled manual workers, those dependent on state pensions, widows without earnings, casual or low-grade workers (DE).

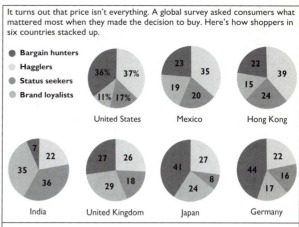

It turns out that price isn't everything. A global survey asked consumers what mattered most when they made the decision to buy. Here's how shoppers in six countries stacked up.

- Bargain hunters
- Hagglers
- Status seekers
- Brand loyalists

United States · Mexico · Hong Kong
India · United Kingdom · Japan · Germany

FIGURE 3.11: What matters to consumers?
Source: Newsweek, 24 July 1995

	Black	Indian Pakistani Bangladeshi	White	Others	Minorities percentage
		thousands			
ENGLAND					
North	5	21	2,988	39	1.3
Yorkshire/Humberside	37	144	4,623	33	4.4
East Midlands	39	120	3,765	29	4.8
East Anglia	14	14	1,984	15	2.1
Greater London	535	521	5,334	290	20.2
Rest of South East	74	170	10,179	104	3.3
South West	22	17	4,547	24	1.4
West Midlands	102	277	4,726	45	8.2
North West	47	147	5,999	50	3.9
WALES	9	16	2,794	16	1.5
SCOTLAND	6	32	4,936	24	1.3
GREAT BRITAIN	891	1,480	51,874	645	5.5

FIGURE 3.12: Ethnic groups, Great Britain, 1991
Source: Social Trends 1994, CSO

ACTIVITY

Study *Fig 3.13* and comment on how different age groups participate in particular sports, games and physical activities. Suggest how a marketing manager might use this information when seeking to introduce a sports or games product in the market.

Percentage in each group participating in each activity in the 12 months before interview

	16-19	20-24	25-29	30-44	45-59	60-69	70 and over	All aged 16 and over	Median age of partici-pants
Walking	72	70	73	73	69	61	37	65	41
Swimming	70	65	63	58	35	20	6	42	34
Snooker, pool, billiards	56	46	37	25	13	7	3	22	29
Keep fit, yoga	31	35	31	23	14	9	5	19	33
Cycling	41	23	22	22	13	8	4	17	35
Darts	29	26	21	15	10	4	2	13	31
Golf	21	19	18	15	11	7	2	12	35
Tenpin bowls, skittles	26	26	19	15	7	2	1	11	30
Running, jogging	30	20	18	13	3	1	-	9	28
Soccer	33	23	18	9	2	-	-	9	25
Weightlifting, training	27	24	20	10	3	-	-	9	27
Badminton	32	18	13	10	4	1	-	9	27
Tennis	29	16	11	9	3	1	-	7	27
Squash	15	15	15	8	2	-	-	6	27
Fishing	11	7	8	8	6	3	1	6	36

FIGURE 3.13: Participation in the most popular sports, games and physical activities, by age, Great Britian, 1990
Source: *Social Trends 1994*, CSO

	Social class				Age					
	AB	C1	C2	DE	16-34	34-64	65 and over	Males	Females	All adults
Percentage of adults holding:										
Building society accounts	78	70	68	49	62	68	62	63	65	65
Bank accounts	94	87	83	66	77	85	77	83	79	81
Premium bonds	45	34	25	15	16	35	34	28	28	28
Unit trusts or investment trusts	19	13	6	2	4	13	7	11	7	9
Shares	27	14	8	4	8	16	9	14	9	12
Government privatisation shares	23	13	7	3	5	14	12	13	8	10
National Savings Bank Investment/ Ordinary account	11	13	10	7	10	10	10	10	10	10
National Savings certificates/bonds	14	12	3	4	5	7	13	8	7	7

FIGURE 3.14: Savings, by social class, age and sex, Great Britain, 1993
Source: *Social Trends 1994*, CSO

The value to organisations of having research information which places people in social classes is that it allows them to make generalisations about the buying behaviour of particular groups, according to their social background. For example, people from different classes show distinct preferences in such areas as newspaper reading, clothing, home furnishing, leisure activities, cars and savings schemes. In the case of savings, this is clearly demonstrated in *Fig 3.14*, which shows that nearly all those in class AB have a bank account compared with only two-thirds in class DE. The difference is even more marked for unit and investment trusts: people in class AB are nearly ten times more likely to hold such investments as those in class DE.

PERSONAL CHARACTERISTICS

To secure a wide picture of purchasing behaviour it is important to gather information on personal factors such as the potential consumer's type of job, economic circumstances, lifestyle and self image. The pattern of demand for, say, clothing is significantly influenced by the type of job that people do. An office worker will buy a formal suit and shirt, a manual worker jeans or overalls.

Consumers' economic circumstances are determined by their level of disposable income and personal wealth, and this has a significant effect on the pattern of demand for a wide range of household goods. Households with less than £100 of disposable income per week spend nearly a quarter of this on food and a further quarter on housing, fuel, light and power. By contrast, those with over £400 of weekly disposable income spend 15 per cent of the total on food and only a further 20 per cent on housing, fuel, light and power. Clearly, the latter group has much more available to spend on luxuries and optional leisure items.

Consumer behaviour is also influenced by **lifestyle**, which reflects consumers' patterns of living as expressed in their activities, interests and opinions. Research into these areas is important for an organisation when dividing the market into segments and identifying target groups. For example, through research, *Lucozade*, which was traditionally sold as a drink to aid recovery from illness, has in recent years extended into another market by being promoted as a sports drink. This has been achieved by suggesting through a range of advertisements that it is an integral part of the lifestyle of such sporting stars as Linford Christie and Daley Thompson.

Research into consumers' self images is important in determining purchasing behaviour. Those who see themselves as being active, sociable and outward going, and are looking for a new car, are likely to be attracted to a make and model advertised by, or associated with, someone sympathetic to that image.

ACTIVITY

Select four advertisements currently being shown on television and identify the type of consumer self image they are associated with.

PSYCHOLOGICAL FACTORS

Organisations need to be sure that their products match the wants of customers and that they are perceived by potential buyers as doing so. Therefore, organisations should understand the psychology of needs and perception.

In *Motivation and Personality* , Abraham Maslow explains why people are motivated by needs which are fundamental to existence and, on the other hand, by those which are associated with mental characteristics or attitudes. Maslow says these needs can be ordered in a hierarchy (see *Fig 3.15*), with people trying progressively to satisfy them.

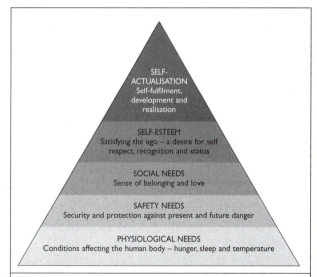

SELF-ACTUALISATION
Self-fulfilment, development and realisation

SELF-ESTEEM
Satisfying the ego – a desire for self respect, recognition and status

SOCIAL NEEDS
Sense of belonging and love

SAFETY NEEDS
Security and protection against present and future danger

PHYSIOLOGICAL NEEDS
Conditions affecting the human body – hunger, sleep and temperature

FIGURE 3.15: Maslow's heirarchy of needs
Source: *Motivation and Personality*, Abraham Maslow

Obviously, any marketing strategy must attempt to link the product or service to the satisfaction of a particular need. For example, in a poor country people may concentrate on the satisfaction of basic physiological needs, such as food, clothing, shelter and warmth. By contrast, in a wealthy economy, many will have moved up the heirarchy to aspire to the ownership of status goods such as fast cars, large houses and swimming pools. They may even be buying camcorders to achieve 'self-actualisation', by expressing their creativity in the making of home videos.

To place a product successfully, it is essential for an organisation to gather market information which accurately identifies the stage at which the majority of potential consumers are in Maslow's heirarchy. It is also important to try to take account of the potential customer's probable perception of the product or service. This is extremely difficult to achieve as it depends on the reaction to information, situations and messages associated with the product or service, some of which will be retained, distorted or rejected. For example, someone actively looking for a new car is more likely to notice advertisements for cars and to retain information about them. However, if someone has already decided which type of car to buy, to reinforce the decision, the person may distort or reject other information.

ASSESSING DEMAND

Knowledge of consumer behaviour and the wider social and commercial environment makes it possible to identify, measure and monitor the factors that influence the demand for products. In addition, there is considerable value to a business organisation in being able to measure and **forecast demand**, as it provides the basis for deciding what markets to enter and which segments to concentrate on. Such measurements and forecasts may be short-term, medium term or long-term; cover from local to world sales; and involve individual products or an entire product range.

The aim is to inform planning. For example, short-term forecasts of demand help in making decisions concerning the optimum purchase of raw materials and components, and the scheduling and financing of production. If the extent of the market is either under-estimated or over-estimated, extra costs may be incurred and profits lost.

MEASUREMENT

Market planning requires the measurement of the total sales of the industry as a whole, the share of sales going to the particular organisation ('market share'), total demand in the market, and the level of demand in particular areas within it.

In the case of **total sales**, information is often available through the industry's trade association or from private market research firms. By expressing its own sales as a percentage of the figure obtained from these sources, it is possible for the organisation to calculate its share of the market.

The **total demand** in the market should be viewed as the total volume that would be purchased at a particular point in time, by a specified consumer group, in a defined geographical area, under particular economic conditions and a defined level of marketing in the industry. One of the most common ways of estimating this level of demand is by taking the number of buyers in the specific market, multiplying this by the quantity purchased by an average buyer in a year, and multiplying the sum by the average price per unit of the product. For example, if the manufacturer of a new type of cola estimates that, within its target market, there are 800,000 potential buyers purchasing on average 75 cans of cola a year at an average price of 50p a can, the total market demand may be valued at £30 million.

The cola manufacturer may initially decide to concentrate its marketing efforts on a particular geographical area. In reaching this decision, it would need to estimate the level of market demand in the area. This is often done by identifying the most important factors influencing the size of the market, such as the percentage of disposable income, total retail sales and population. The relative importance of the factors is then assessed and weighted by use of a multiplier (if factor X is regarded as twice as significant as factor Y, the former will be multiplied by a value double that for factor Y). A calculation can then be made to project the buying power of the locality.

To take an example: if a food chain was expanding to operate nationally, it would study the relative buying power of different geographical areas before deciding where to locate new outlets. One of the areas might be Westshire. This has 0.05 per cent of the nation's disposable income, 0.08 per cent of retail sales and 0.055 per cent of the population. If income were weighted as the most important factor at 0.5, retail sales next at 0.3 and population at 0.2, the following sum could be compiled to determine the size of the Westshire market: $(0.5 \times 0.05) + (0.3 \times 0.08) + (0.2 \times 0.055) = 0.06$ per cent of national buying power. If the organisation estimated that total national sales could reach £1 billion, those in Westshire could be expected to be valued at £600,000. Figures for areas could be compared in reaching a decision about the locations for expansion. However, the accuracy and value of this kind of calculation depend upon the weights selected and the quality of statistics used.

FORECASTING

Forecasting involves predictions about how buyers may behave in future in a specified set of circumstances. A general approach that can be taken to **sales forecasting** involves three stages. A company makes an economic forecast as to the future levels of gross domestic product; applies this and a number of other indicators in estimating future sales in the industry; and bases the forecast for its own sales on the assumption that it will achieve a certain proportion of the industry's total.

There are a number of other approaches that can be taken to sales forecasting. First, it is possible to carry out a survey of potential buyers' future intentions and determine the probability of a particular group of people buying a product in the future. Second, it is possible to carry out a survey of expert opinion within the industry. This could involve contacting sales representatives, suppliers, distributors and trade associations to build up a picture of what they think might happen in the future. Such an approach is often taken by car producers, who survey their dealers in order to forecast short-term demand. Third, a statistical method known as time series analysis enables long-term movements to be charted, offering a relatively sound basis for making projections.

ACTIVITY

A chain of sports shops has estimated that total UK sales could reach £2 bn. The company is considering the possibility of expanding its operation into either Middleshire or Wilburyshire.

Research has provided the following figures: Middleshire: percentage of national disposable income 0.07 per cent, of retail sales 0.08 per cent, and of population 0.085 per cent; and for Wilburyshire 0.12 per cent, 0.06 per cent and 0.075 per cent, respectively.

In terms of national buying power the relative importance of these factors is weighted thus: income 0.3, population 0.45 and retail sales 0.25. Calculate the sales potential of the two areas.

RESEARCH METHODS

There are essentially two research methods, desk research and field research.

DESK RESEARCH

This involves using existing research information, which may be internal or external to the organisation. In the case of the former, it may include information about accounts, invoices, stock control levels and sales. For example, the organisation's own records of past sales may provide valuable data by which to establish a connection between the company's performance and outside influences.

There are many external sources of information, including volumes of annual statistics published by the Central Statistical Office (CSO), of which the *Annual Abstract of Statistics*, the *Family Expenditure Survey, Regional Trends* and *Social Trends* are among the most useful. They provide data on broad aggregates in the economy such as national income and expenditure, industrial production, investment, international trade, prices and information on demographic and social trends. In addition to the CSO, the Office of Population Censuses and Surveys (OPCS) provides demographic and other census-related data. In all, the government publishes 400 series of statistics. A guide to sources of government statistics is published annually (*Government Statistics: a brief guide to sources*, available free on request from: Central Statistical Office, Press, Publications and Publicity, Great George Street, London SWIP 3AQ).

Other sources are trade publications, directories and magazines, which specialise in collecting market data in a particular business sector. These contain data, information and articles on subjects and developments of relevance to the industry, as well as expert opinion on the effects of political, economic and social trends. Two trade sources especially worth noting are the Joint Industry Committee for Television Audience Research, which produces weekly figures on commercial television audience levels, and the Audit Bureau of Circulation, which provides audited information on newspaper and magazine sales. Also useful are the journals of professional associations and institutions. If these are read in conjunction with news media such as *The Economist, Management Today, Marketing Week, Marketing* and the *Financial Times*, a good overview can be obtained of developments in the business world.

INFORMATION TECHNOLOGY

The rapid growth of information technology has made research data much more accessible and easier to analyse. This is due to the ever-increasing processing power of computers and developments, such as broadband technology, which enable large amounts of information to be moved rapidly around the world. For the first time, it is becoming possible - and commercially viable in terms of cost - to access and analyse data which previously was either too remote or could only be obtained in a predigested and simplified form. Information technology also enables data to be made available more quickly; no longer do users have to wait for printed volumes to appear. As a result, by being more up to date, information provides a more reliable basis on which to make decisions and gives an earlier indication of developments which may have commercial significance, enabling an organisation to react more quickly.

Among new developments, the use of the Internet to access data sources world wide and the use of census data for 'community profiling' are worth particular note. Since 1991, census data are available by enumeration district as well as by local government ward and county. As an enumeration district comprises no more than 200 households, use of these data provides the opportunity to construct detailed profiles of local communities. 'Community profiling' can also be achieved by analysing data by post code.

Another significant development is the computerised model of the economy developed for H. M. Treasury. This enables fairly accurate forecasts of what is likely to happen in terms of the major economic indicators, such as income, expenditure, output, employment, growth, inflation and the balance of payments. It allows many larger companies to monitor movements in their own markets by putting market research information through the computer to analyse present and possible future trends.

BENEFITS OF DESK RESEARCH

Desk research is economical and comparatively speedy, and it has the advantage that it can be conducted with complete confidentiality, i.e. without competitors finding out! On the other hand, because the information was not generated for the particular purposes of the organisation, it may not be sufficiently relevant. Field research may be required to supplement it.

FIELD RESEARCH

When existing sources of information have been tapped, it may be necessary to supplement them by fresh enquiries, such as through the use of surveys or focus discussion groups. This enables organisations to make direct contact with potential or actual customers, and to ask them questions specific to the organisation's needs. Original research yields primary data (secondary data are found in existing sources).

Surveys may be based on a questionnaire which is conducted as part of an interview, or through a discussion group, or by post or over the telephone. Generally it is too expensive and time consuming to contact every potential customer, so only a sample of customers is included in the survey. This sample has to be very carefully selected.

SAMPLING

The vast majority of people do not intentionally distort their answers in responding to a questionnaire, but the conclusions drawn from research will not be reliable if the consumer sample used is not representative of the market being investigated.

Reliability relates to probability and the concept derives from the fact that surveys are usually carried out using only a small number (or 'sample') of the population to which the findings will be applied. When political pollsters want to find out the popularity of the government, they choose just one or two thousand people to ask, but they use the answers to make general statements about the electorate as a whole. Whether their conclusions are sound or not depends, among other things, on the extent to which error has been contained so that users can confidently rely on the accuracy of the findings. The reliability of data depends on the size of the sample group – is it big enough to enable valid conclusions to be drawn based on its opinions? – and the extent to which its composition is representative of the wider population to which the findings will be applied.

To ensure that a survey sample is **representative**, researchers first determine the wider population (or 'universe', as they call it). They then work out the size of

the sample. If it is too small, reliability may suffer; if it is too large, unnecessary cost will be incurred. Ideally, the sample should be a small mirror image of the 'universe', in terms of its relevant characteristics, which may include gender, ethnicity, age, marital status, location, class, and so on.

The larger the number of sub-groups within the 'universe' that a researcher wishes to find out about, the larger the sample that is required. For example, if the 'universe' is estimated at one million people and the consumer sample consists of 3,000, a sub-group of the 'universe' which is only two per cent of the 'universe' will comprise 60 people in the sample. This may be too few to give an accurate indication of opinions held by the wider group which they are supposed to represent. For example, in a survey of 2,000 people, representative of the population as a whole, just over half of these will be women, but fewer than 150 will be women in their twenties and maybe no more than a dozen will be women in their twenties who live in Scotland. Two ways of tackling this problem are to create an overall bigger sample or to increase the number in the particular sub-group (although this must be taken into account when analysing the results as a whole).

Having decided upon the size of the sample, the researcher chooses a method for selecting those who will comprise it. There are four approaches.

The **probability** system involves obtaining a list of the 'universe' to be researched. Names and addresses may be available from trade and telephone directories, the electoral register, magazine subscription lists and membership lists of professional and voluntary organisations, among others. The researcher may take one name in 30 from the lists and allocate them to interviewers. They, in turn, will need to ensure that, as they conduct interviews, a representative cross-section is achieved. Inevitably, this means some of the people who have been interviewed will have to be rejected, otherwise bias may develop within the sample.

The **random selection** system involves contacting households on an speculative basis. The interviewer selects contacts by requesting the cooperation of passers-by, perhaps asking every tenth person until someone consents to be interviewed. Random selection is more acceptable than the interviewer being allowed to decide, as it prevents personal preferences coming into play. The composition of the survey group may, to some extent, be predetermined by basing the random selection upon homes which can be placed into sub-groups. For example, areas may be placed into categories in terms of regions, rural or urban location, and types of dwelling. This may be especially useful when the sample is to contain sub-groups based upon such characteristics.

The **quota** system is a very popular method of consumer research because it can be clearly defined. Once the size of the sample is decided, the sub-groups are defined and interviewers are allocated a quota of individuals which they must contact according to certain characteristics of the sub-groups. For example, an interviewer may be required to trace and interview a certain number of households which are owner occupiers, include two children of school age, where both parents work, and which are urban.

The **consumer panel** involves establishing a panel of households which acts as a representative sample of the market. Panel members are asked to provide regular details of their spending, identifying products, prices and sizes, the place and time of purchase or similar information. Such panels are expensive to establish and require continuing attention if they are to be maintained sufficiently long to make the results worthwhile. The longer a household remains on the panel, the more accustomed it becomes to making returns. It may then become less self-conscious when making purchases, ceasing to consider the implications they will have on its consumer report. It may then act more naturally in accordance with its personal tastes and preferences, and thus the information submitted to the researcher will be more valuable.

ACTIVITY

Consider the most appropriate method of sampling to employ when conducting surveys of political voting intentions and of household expenditure.

QUESTIONNAIRE DESIGN

The success of a sample survey depends to a large extent upon the quality of the questionnaire used. Questions should be designed so that the answers allow respondents to be classified into the required sub-groups of the 'universe'.

Initial questions usually seek personal facts about the respondent, such as marital status, age group and occupation. Some of these questions may be designed to stimulate the interviewee's interest in the survey and create an impression that the person's contribution is important for the research. Questions of a more deeply personal nature, required to identify sub-groups in terms of income and spending habits, can follow later when the respondent has become more relaxed.

Although the majority of people will have no reason for giving false information, many may hesitate to divulge information which could show them in an unfavourable

light. Where such questions are necessary, the responses given can be checked against those to similar questions, placed elsewhere in the questionnaire. This enables the researcher to test the **validity** of the interviewee's response.

A questionnaire comprising highly structured questions, possible answers to which have been classified into predetermined categories, is quick to administer and the resulting data easy to process. By contrast, a questionnaire comprising open-ended questions creates problems of interpretation and analysis, as well as in recording data.

When writing questions, several points should be taken into account.

QUESTIONNAIRES SHOULD...

1 **Use simple language**

2 **Have clear meaning**

3 **Be administered neutrally**

4 **Avoid leading questions**

5 **Keep questions brief**

6 **Avoid embarrassing questions**

7 **Avoid two-part questions**

8 **Be expressed in positive language**

ACTIVITY

What's wrong with the following questions?

'Have you travelled to France by ferry or through the rail tunnel?'

'Do you clean your car regularly?'

'Which type of car, like Ford or Vauxhall, do you feel is the most reliable?'

SURVEY METHODS

The **personal interview** is generally regarded as the most effective method of conducting a survey as it produces the best response. A personable and experienced interviewer acquires a technique which encourages participation and results in completer and more accurate answers. The interviewer can put the person being interviewed at ease; the value of participation can be explained; and any difficulties in understanding can be overcome by rephasing questions. Where the quota system is used, the interviewer will gain experience of certain types of household and be more readily able to identify areas where they can be located. The interviewer may also become accomplished in identifying general characteristics of individuals or households, so that questionnaire responses may be supplemented by additional information.

Personal interviews are an expensive method of conducting surveys, given the time and expenses involved. This is particularly the case where the probability and random selection systems are used, which involve revisits to respondents not initially at home. Similarly, in the quota system, a sub-group may have characteristics which makes it time-consuming and difficult to trace individuals within a particular area, and this, too, adds to costs. If questionnaires are completed face to face, there is the danger that interviewees may try to give the answers expected of them, or those they believe will create the best impression.

Postal surveys are less expensive but the response rate is poor, which means large numbers of questionnaires have to be mailed to obtain a sufficient number of replies. Because there is no interviewer on hand to assist those filling them in, mail questionnaires must be especially well laid out and questions and instructions clearly expressed and in plain language. The method of answering the questions should reduce the effort involved to a minimum, for example by using ticks and crosses or circling items. Higher response rates to mail questionnaires may be achieved if a covering letter makes an appeal for participation and, perhaps, explains the purpose of the research and its use. Also, people are more likely to respond when they feel an affiliation with the purpose; for example, it is a subject they feel strongly about. However, this can introduce fresh problems in terms of the representativeness of the responses received.

Over 85 per cent of UK households have a telephone, and conducting **interviews by phone** is less expensive than personal interviewing and more likely to elicit a response than use of a mail questionnaire. However, there is a danger that bias may enter the responses if it is found that only a certain type of person is willing to provide personal information to an unknown and unseen caller.

Discussion groups bring together a representative group of people to express their tastes and preferences in relation to certain products or to give their views in general on household consumer items. The person conducting the meeting will be an experienced researcher able to

	Personal interview	Postal survey	Phone survey	Discussion group
Interviewer bias				
Depth of questioning				
Cost				
Speed in obtaining response				
Flexibility				
Control over data collected				

ACTIVITY

Rank the different survey methods with a score of one (low) to four (high) in terms of their advantages and disadvantages.

create an atmosphere in which the participants feel free to express their opinions. The researcher will introduce topics and guide the conversation. The whole exercise may be filmed or recorded for subsequent analysis, including of tone and strength of expression and body language. In some cases, a group of researchers is hidden behind a glass wall, so that they can follow the proceedings without being seen. They can then relay information to the researcher with the group, including conversational leads that should be followed up. Usually, respondents selected to take part in focus discussion groups are paid to attend. There is the danger that, in a small group, one or two people will try to dominate, but an effective researcher knows how to handle this, and to 'bring out' the less forthcoming members.

TEST MARKETING

When a large capital investment is involved in the development of a new or improved product, some form of test marketing will generally be an important pre-condition for a national sales effort. Test marketing applies not only to the product but also to all the marketing activities supporting it, namely the sales organisation, the distribution system and advertising and promotional aspects. It allows the company to experience the realities of competitive pressures in a market, to discover any deficiencies and to modify the product and the arrangements. Test marketing has an impressive record:

about 90 per cent of products subsequently launched nationally are successful.

When conducting market testing it is important to ensure that several conditions apply. One is that the test area must be sufficiently large and have the required characteristics to make it representative of the marketing 'universe', so that results can be a reliable guide in selling the product to a wider public. Another is that, if the effect of advertising is being assessed, the product test area should, as nearly as possible, coincide with the readership areas of the local media.

Test marketing should not attempt to assess too many factors at the same time in the same area, as it will be difficult to disentangle the various effects. For example, if the effectiveness of promotional activities is being assessed, altering other aspects, such as packaging and price, will tend only to confuse the issue. The response of competitors should be monitored, to judge whether any competition is local in nature or could be repeated and sustained nationally.

The length of the test period should be long enough to provide evidence of seasonal fluctuations in demand as well as to enable confirmation of initial findings. The test area should be kept under scrutiny even after the product has been launched to a wider public. This may provide early warning of problems which may arise only after the product has been available for a while.

PORTFOLIO ASSIGNMENT

SCHOOL OR COLLEGE SHOP SURVEY

The governors of your school or college are looking at a number of ways of raising funds. One involves buying a mobile building for use as a student shop. Your business studies group has been asked to conduct the initial market research, to test the feasibility of the idea.

Design a questionnaire to determine whether there is a need for a shop; who would use it and how much they would be likely to spend in it; what items the shop should stock; its opening times and location.

Compare your questionnaire with those designed by other students, then, working as a team, create a final version and conduct a survey throughout your school or college.

Write a report to the governors, presenting the findings, drawing conclusions and making recommendations. Your report should also describe the survey methods used and assess the accuracy of the findings.

PORTFOLIO ASSIGNMENT

TEENAGE MAGAZINE

Eastern Press publishes a number of successful women's magazines and a weekly publication listing television programmes. Now, the company wants to extend its range of publications by moving into the older teenage market. In particular, it wants to assess whether there is sufficient demand for a new title among 16-19 year-olds of both sexes and with an ABC social background.

The company's inclination is that the magazine should be weekly and cover areas such as music, sport, fashion and beauty, television and cinema, careers and higher education, social and political issues, and fiction. It should also include competitions and carry a pull-out poster. However, the editorial development team has few ideas about price, format, design, promotion and distribution of the magazine.

You work for a market research agency specialising in the magazine industry, and have been asked to investigate the feasibility of Eastern Press's idea.

Design a suitable questionnaire and conduct a survey which will allow you to confirm or reject Eastern Press's ideas. The survey should be based on a sample of 50 students at your school or college.

Eastern Press also wants to be reassured that this is the right time to be moving into such a new venture. Find out more by using secondary data.

Combine your findings in a report which also explains the methods used. Prepare a verbal presentation of your conclusions and recommendations. This is to be made to the directors of Eastern Press (your tutors/teachers).

Marketing communications and target audiences

THE BASIS FOR MARKETING COMMUNICATIONS

Effective communication involves the exchange of information to achieve mutual understanding and, perhaps, to promote action. In marketing, it centres on the use of advertising, public relations, sales promotions and direct marketing activities. The aim is to influence purchasing decisions, in particular as made by specific consumer groups (or 'target audiences'). A secondary aim is to obtain beneficial publicity for the organisation so as to enhance its public image.

For marketing communications to be effective, the **target audience** should comprise a group of consumers who are sufficiently alike to suggest that its members will respond in a similar way to a particular advertisement or other promotional 'message'.

ACTIVITY

The new Ford Probe is described as a 2 + 2 coupé with a choice of two engines, a sports 2.0 litre, 16-valve, double-overhead camshaft, four cylinder engine with an output of 115 PS or a refined 2.5 litre, 24-valve, four-cam V6 engine with an output of 165 PS. Both are mounted transversely and drive the front wheels through a manual five-speed close ratio transmission.

Consider the market segment that Ford would want to inform about the availability of this product.

STAGES AND TYPES

The targeted consumer requires three types of information before making a purchasing decision. The potential buyer needs to know:

- **that the product exists and where it can be bought;**

- **descriptive details about it; and**

- **information useful in evaluating the product in relation to the prospective customer's needs.**

All these types of information have to pass through a number of **stages of communication**, namely origination, choice of format, choice of channel and receipt by members of the intended audience.

One of the practical problems associated with this sequence is that it is essentially one way and offers little opportunity for feedback. This makes it difficult to measure the effectiveness of marketing communications other than by the use of such broad indicators as a comparison of sales before and after an advertising campaign.

Another problem arises from the need for organisations to take account of other communications which they do not control. For example, some consumers may act as opinion leaders, influencing the views of others by making recommendations and giving advice. Such people are generally recognised by their peers because they are considered to have expert knowledge on a particular product or service. For a marketing communication to be effective, it must be received and accepted by these opinion formers. Organisations also have to pay attention to the various sources of impartial consumer advice which come from consumer group reports, newspaper articles and material issued by government agencies. These may support or damage the marketing communication put out by the organisation.

There are two types of communication that are controlled by the organisation. One is **impersonal** in that it is aimed at providing information to a large number of people, for example an advertising campaign in the mass media. This may be appropriate for a high volume consumer product such as a new washing powder or soft drink, where the primary aim is to provide information about the existence of the product to as many people as possible. The other is **personal**, involving the supply of information directly to individuals by personal, postal or phone contact. This approach is often regarded as appropriate where the targeted consumer is taking a relatively large purchasing decision, as when buying a house or car.

In certain cases, it is appropriate to use both types of communication. For example, an organisation which is responsible for designing and building new conservatories may initially run an advertising campaign in appropriate magazines or newspapers and follow up any enquiries with a visit by a consultant or sales person.

ACTIVITY

Identify the major types of music purchased by the members of your class or group.

List the impersonal and personal ways in which the music industry communicates its market message. Does this vary with the type of music? How effective is it?

Identify the 'opinion leaders' in your class or group. Why are they viewed as such? How do they keep themselves up to date with what is happening in the music industry?

Identify the sources of impartial advice available to consumers of music products.

ADVERTISING

Advertising is an impersonal form of communication. It involves the use of communications media to inform, persuade, publicise and remind potential and existing consumers about an organisation's products and activities. Essentially, it is a means of increasing sales. It

may also be used to encourage consumers to purchase products or services from a particular retail outlet. The following panel gives a list of reasons for advertising.

ADVERTISING OBJECTIVES

⊗ **Promote and establish an image for the organisation and its products.**

⊗ **Tell potential buyers about a new product and to encourage them to buy it.**

⊗ **Increase sales by reminding potential and existing consumers about its products and activities.**

⊗ **Undermine the potential buyer's loyalty towards competing products.**

⊗ **Provide technical and general information about the product or service.**

⊗ **Focus on the unique selling points of a product.**

⊗ **Provide details of special offers, samples, brochures or promotions.**

⊗ **Generate initial enquiries that the sales force may follow up.**

⊗ **Encourage retailers or wholesalers to stock the product.**

THE ADVERTISING CAMPAIGN

Advertising is an important part of an organisation's promotional activities. An advertising campaign must be carefully planned, with a clear view as to whether the retailer or the consumer is to be targeted and whether it is the product or the organisation which is to be promoted.

The effectiveness of advertising is often increased if the product or organisation already has a strong brand identity. This means that it has a readily recognised name, sign, logo or design. Examples are many, including Levi's jeans, Hoover vacuum cleaners and BMW cars. High levels of recognition mean that the organisation can promote its products and publicise its activities to good effect by using these devices on sales literature, delivery vehicles, stationery or point of sale displays

Many medium sized and large organisations seek the specialist services of an advertising agency. Agencies provide expert advice and carry out or manage a number of tasks, including copywriting; design and layout, including use of type, style and visual matter; film production for television or cinema use; space buying in media and other outlets, such as billboards; and evaluation.

The most successful agencies are those able clearly to identify the needs of an organisation and to translate them into effective advertisements. In selecting an agency, it may be helpful to follow the advice of the Advertising Association or the Institute of Practitioners in Advertising.

Any advertising campaign has to adhere to a usually strict budget, the size of which will be determined, at least ideally, by several factors. These include the objectives of the campaign (what the organisation intends to achieve by it); the amount competitors are spending in promoting their products; and the stage the product has reached in its life cycle. Spending on the advertising of a product is generally high when it is launched, relatively steady during its maturity, and ceases in its period of decline.

One of the major decisions associated with an advertising campaign concerns **choice of media**. Channels of communication include newspapers, magazines, television and radio, cinema, and outdoor displays. To ensure that the market place is adequately covered, it is often appropriate to use a mix of media. Details about sources of advertising media, classified by area, price and potential audience, can be found in the BRAD (British Rate and Data) directory.

ACTIVITY

Select an advertisement from a weekly consumer magazine and answer the following questions:

⊗ **What are the main objectives of the advertiser?**

⊗ **What is the target audience?**

⊗ **How does the advertisement use images, design, colour and text to achieve its purposes?**

NEWSPAPERS

Britain has a large coverage of national tabloid and broadsheet newspapers, with a daily readership of more than 27 million, rising to 31 million on Sundays, in 1992 (see *Fig 3.16*). The most popular daily is *The Sun,* which is

	Percentage of adults reading each paper in 1992			Percentage of adults reading each paper in 1992				Readership (millions)		Readers per copy (numbers)
	Males	Females	All adults	15-24	25-44	45-64	65 and over	1971	1992	1992
Daily newspapers										
The Sun	24	19	21	28	23	20	15	8.5	9.7	2.7
Daily Mirror	19	15	17	18	16	18	17	13.8	7.8	2.8
Daily Mail	10	10	10	8	9	11	11	4.8	4.5	2.6
Daily Express	9	8	8	7	6	10	11	9.7	3.8	2.5
The Daily Telegraph	6	5	6	4	4	7	7	3.6	2.5	2.4
Daily Star	7	4	5	8	6	5	2	.	2.4	3.0
Today	4	3	3	4	4	3	2	.	1.5	2.9
The Guardian	3	2	3	3	4	3	1	1.1	1.3	3.1
The Independent	3	2	2	2	3	2	1	.	1.1	2.9
The Times	3	2	2	2	2	3	1	1.1	1.0	2.7
Financial Times	2	1	1	1	2	1	.	0.7	0.6	3.6
Any national daily newspaper	65	56	60	59	57	64	62	.	27.3	.
Sunday newspapers										
News of the World	29	26	28	35	31	26	19	15.8	12.5	2.7
Sunday Mirror	20	18	19	22	20	20	16	13.5	8.8	3.2
The People	14	13	13	13	12	15	14	14.4	6.1	2.9
The Mail on Sunday	13	13	13	14	14	14	9	.	5.8	2.9
Sunday Express	11	11	11	10	8	13	14	10.4	4.9	2.8
The Sunday Times	9	7	8	9	9	8	4	3.7	3.5	3.0
Sunday Telegraph	4	4	4	3	4	5	5	2.1	1.8	3.2
The Observer	4	3	4	4	4	4	2	2.4	1.7	3.1
Sunday Sport	5	1	3	7	3	1	.	.	1.3	4.1
Independent on Sunday	3	2	3	4	4	2	1	.	1.3	3.2
Any Sunday newspaper	71	67	69	71	68	72	66	.	31.3	.

FIGURE 3.16: Readership of national newspapers, by sex and age, Great Britain, 1992

Note: Readership is defined as the average issue readership and represents the number of people who claim to have read or looked at one or more copies of a given publication during the period equal to the interval at which the publication appears.

Source: *Social Trends 1994*, CSO

read by one in four men and one in five women. On Sundays, 12 million read *The News of the World*.

Age is a significant indicator of readership, for example 25 per cent of those aged 15-24 read *The Sun* compared to 15 per cent of those over 65. Since 1971, new titles have come onto the market, including *The Independent* and *Today*. Sales of the former shows a noted gender bias, with five per cent of men but only one per cent of women reading it.

This sort of information helps to determine where an advertisement should be placed so as to have the most impact on its target audience. Advertising agencies can give advice by providing **readership profiles** for newspapers which identify typical buyers in terms of social class and income. Also, newspapers themselves give advice on the best days to place advertisements. For example, it is generally thought that mail order items should be advertised at the weekend because this is when people have the leisure to browse advertisements.

Regional and local free newspapers also provide extensive coverage. They often group advertisements in classified sections. This means advertisers can be confident that their advertisement will be read by those who are most interested.

MAGAZINES

Britain has a wide range of magazines aimed at the mass market, including many that target women. Again, considerable variations exist in the age and gender of readerships (see *Fig 3.17*). Incidentally, the large number of television listings magazines have come into being since the end of the BBC's monopoly, in 1991, on the publication of its own listings.

As for newspapers, advertising agencies can give advice on readership profiles and supply details of other types of magazines, such as those produced by professional associations, those aimed at particular retail and trade groups and those covering specialist hobby and leisure interests. One of the major advantages of placing an advertisement in a magazine, rather than a newspaper, is that the publication is likely to have a longer 'life': it may be re-read over many months and seen by many more people among the target audience.

	Percentage of adults reading each magazine in 1992			Percentage of each age group reading each magazine in 1992				Readership (millions)		Readers per copy (numbers)
	Males	Females	All adults	15-24	25-44	45-64	65 and over	1971	1992	1992
General magazines:										
Reader's Digest	14	12	13	9	12	17	14	9.2	5.9	3.9
Radio Times	13	12	12	14	12	13	12	9.5	5.7	3.6
TV Times	11	11	11	15	10	11	9	9.9	5.0	4.5
Viz	14	5	10	29	11	2	.	.	4.3	1.0
TV Quick	5	8	6	9	8	5	3	.	2.9	.
What's on TV	6	7	6	9	7	4	5	.	2.8	1.9
Women's magazines										
Bella	3	14	9	10	11	8	7	.	3.3	.
Women's Own	3	14	9	10	10	8	7	7.2	3.4	4.9
Take a Break	4	13	8	12	10	8	4	.	3.0	.
Woman	2	11	6	6	7	6	5	8.0	2.6	3.8
Woman's Weekly	2	10	6	3	4	7	11	4.7	2.4	3.2
Best	2	10	6	7	7	6	3	.	2.3	3.9

FIGURE 3.17: Readership of the most popular magazines, by sex and age, 1992
Source: *Social Trends 1994*, CSO

ACTIVITY

Collect a range of daily, Sunday and local newspapers, together with examples of general and specialist magazines.

Study the publications and the types of advertisements they contain.

Discuss the probable target audience for each publication and complete the readership profile below.

Use the readership profile to decide where best to place advertisements for these products:

- ✪ a new record by East 17
- ✪ an all-timber conservatory
- ✪ a coach tour to Scotland
- ✪ bottom of the range kitchen units
- ✪ a hedge trimmer
- ✪ a second-hand car
- ✪ expensive jewellery
- ✪ oven ready chips
- ✪ vintage port
- ✪ a pension plan
- ✪ holiday flats in Spain

TITLE OF PUBLICATION	CHARACTERISTICS			
	Age	Gender	Class	Significant other

TELEVISION

The vast majority of households have television, making it an important advertising medium. It is particularly attractive to advertisers as it allows a combination of music, speech and pictures, as well as the use of jingles, well-known personalities and mini-dramas as aids to the creation of brand interest and identity.

The effectiveness of television advertising depends on a large number of the target group of consumers watching the advertisement at the same time. Therefore, its placement in an appropriate programme slot is vital. 'Prime time' programmes, especially soap operas, provide some of the most 'penetrative' opportunities for advertising to a mass market. The link between popular programmes and advertising markets was demonstrated, in 1994, by the decision of ITV to advertise certain programmes, including *Coronation Street*, in particular trade magazines, for example *Cracker* in *The Grocer* and *The Bill* in *Publican and Off-Licence News*.

The growth in the number of television channels has tended to spread the viewing audience across a wider range of programmes. This makes it more difficult to target a particular market segment. The situation has been complicated still further by the widespread ownership of video cassette recorders, which enable people both to 'self-schedule' television and 'fast forward' through advertisements (see panel).

The effectiveness of newspaper and television advertisements is monitored weekly in the Adwatch survey and reported in *Marketing*. A sample of 500 or more adults is asked to rank advertisements according to the frequency they remember having seen or heard them in a period.

LIVE VIEWING

Using the video to self-schedule TV programmes remains largely the province of young ABC1s, according to research by TGI (see *Fig 3.18*).

Asked whether they agreed with the statement that TV programmes are preferable 'live' rather than on video, it was the young and upwardly mobile who were more likely to reach for their remote controls.

The highest agreement index in favour of 'live' TV was among the 65-plus age band, probably because they spend more time in the house and in front of the box.

Similarly, women generally, and housewives specifically, had a higher index of agreement with the statement because they are more likely to be in the house to watch it at the time it is screened.

The highest index is among the E demograph, partly attributable to a higher proportion of unemployment and lower income levels causing them to spend more time in the home.

The lowest index of agreement is at the other end of the spectrum, with ABs having more cash, more leisure time outside the home, and more of a need to use the video.

From a buyer's point of view this excerbates the difficulty of reaching ABC1 males who, if they are recording, are probably zipping through the ads.

But it is children under 14 who agree most strongly with the statement that video scheduling is best, largely because [it means] they don't watch with their parents over their shoulders.

From *Marketing*, 1 December 1994

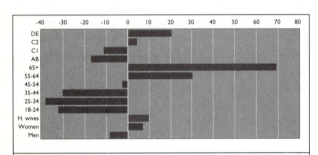

FIGURE 3.18: Who watches 'live' television?

ACTIVITY

Design a suitable questionnaire and conduct a survey to find out the best remembered advertisements among the students in your school or college.

Compare the results with those appearing in the current edition of *Marketing*. Account for, and comment on, any significant differences.

RADIO

Radio provides a local and, increasingly, a national medium for placing advertisements, particularly those aimed at 16-24 year-olds. In 1994, commercial radio accounted for four per cent of radio audiences and generated a revenue of £219m. Three stations – Virgin, Classic FM and Atlantic 252 – accounted for 22 per cent of total commercial radio hours.

Radio is a rapidly growing advertising medium and has the advantage over television of having much lower production costs. Local radio can help to develop a strong community feeling which small local businesses may benefit from in buying advertising.

CINEMA

The introduction of multi-screen cinemas and the consequent revival in cinema attendance has benefited advertising in the 1990s. Cinemas provide advertisers with a captive audience which can be reached relatively cheaply. As a medium, it is of particular value to local retailers, businesses, hotels and restaurants.

OUTDOOR DISPLAYS

Use may be made of parking meters, sandwich boards, taxis, buses and tube trains, telephone kiosks, hoardings and flashing signs.

GUIDELINES AND CONTROLS

The Advertising Standards Authority (ASA) is the body which regulates the UK advertising industry. The advertising profession has adopted a code of practice which the ASA administers for all non-broadcast media. The code aims to ensure that advertisements provide a fair, honest and unambiguous representation of the products they promote, including through the use of words and impressions.

The ASA gives guidance to advertisers on whether a proposed advertisement would be regarded as acceptable and deals with complaints from the general public about cases of allegedly untruthful, misleading or offensive advertisements.

The ASA is not an enforcement agency and operates on a voluntary basis. Any breaches of the law are generally referred to the Office of Fair Trading. Following an investigation the ASA can request an advertiser to amend or withdraw an unsuitable advertisement. On the rare occasion an advertiser refuses, the ASA may seek to put pressure on the offending advertiser through the Committee of Advertising Practice (CAP), which is made up of organisations representing all areas of the media, including advertisers and advertising agency associations. The ASA can issue a warning to CAP members and, as they are not supposed to accept advertisements which breach the code, this would make it difficult for the offending advertiser to continue to buy space. However, if the advertisement is still being run, the ASA can fall back on the Control of Misleading Advertisements Regulations 1988, referring the advertisement to the Office of Fair Trading.

In the case of television advertising, there are four groups that act as watchdogs over standards.

- ☻ **The Broadcast Complaints Commission is a statutory body which deals with any complaints of unjust or unfair treatment. It has no disciplinary powers.**

- ☻ **The Broadcasting Standards Council is a statutory body dealing with issues of sex, violence, taste or decency. It also has no disciplinary powers.**

- ☻ **The Independent Television Commission is also a statutory body, set up to regulate commercial television, which monitors the use of advertisements and can enforce action, where necessary.**

- ☻ **The Broadcasting Advertising Clearance Centre is run by the ITV Centre and vets all advertising copy before it is screened.**

PUBLIC RELATIONS

Public relations is a means of publicising and promoting an organisation's image with a view to influencing customers to buy products, investors to buy shares and government and others to act in ways helpful to the organisation. Essentially, it involves impersonal types of communication. In many cases it consists in the placement of information about the organisation in a suitable publication or obtaining a favourable presentation of its activities on radio, television or elsewhere without this having to be paid for. The following panel lists reasons for carrying out public relations.

PUBLIC RELATIONS OBJECTIVES

- ☻ **Promote confidence in, and create a favourable image of, a product or organisation in the eyes of the general public, bankers, customers and suppliers.**

- ☻ **Increase understanding of an organisation, its scope and products.**

- ☻ **Bring the organisation and its**

---

products to the attention of those it wishes to reach, and to do so beneficially.

- ☻ **Generate more business and profits.**

THE PUBLIC RELATIONS CAMPAIGN

Strengths
Weaknesses
Opportunities
Threats

In designing a public relations campaign it is useful to conduct a SWOT analysis to put the organisation and its products into perspective. This will help to highlight the main internal strengths and weaknesses of the organisation, together with any external opportunities and threats. It may be that an organisation has strengths in research development and the use of new technologies, but it suffers from weaknesses in management and labour turnover. Opportunities may be opening up in European markets; on the other hand, there may be threats from American competition. Under these circumstances, it is important to publicise the organisation's strengths and to play down any perceived weaknesses.

In addition, the findings from a SWOT analysis allow the organisation to identify the people and groups which may influence the attitudes and views of others, such as academic and commercial research organisations; management groups; existing, past and future customers; newspapers, radio and television; major suppliers; and European, national or local government officials. The public relations team should be in regular contact with these groups in order to influence their views as, ultimately, they affect the opinions of others.

Organisations, or the agencies they hire, may decide to use one or more of a number of activities in a public relations campaign.

1. **Press releases** may be issued to draw attention to the successes of the organisation. These might include an announcement concerning the creation of a new product, success in securing a new order, or some other development or achievement. An advantage of a press release is that it offers the organisation's version of a particular event (and, of course, it is free).

2. **Briefing** may be provided for those who will speak on the organisation's behalf, whether an employee or someone from outside the organisation, to ensure that the organisation's case is presented effectively on television and radio and at events. Similarly, public appearances or speeches can be used to provide opportunities to promote the name and activities of an organisation. This may involve television and radio appearances as well as local activities such as giving a speech at a chamber of commerce lunch.

3. **Sponsorship** may be offered to have the name of an organisation linked to a particular event. Examples include the Coca-Cola Cup, the Lombard RAC Rally and the Benson & Hedges Cup (cricket). Small local businesses can gain from sponsoring charity fundraising events, local sports clubs (with kit) or cultural events, such as helping to finance a theatre production. In every case, it is a matter of having the name of the organisation publicised and placed in a favourable light.

ACTIVITY

List all the sporting, cultural or general entertainment events that you can think of which are sponsored. In each case, identify what is the probable benefit for the organisation concerned.

SALES PROMOTION

A sales promotion is an attempt to communicate directly with potential consumers or distributors in order to encourage them to purchase or stock the product or service as well as to recommend it to others. It may involve both impersonal and, in some cases, personal channels of communication.

Consumer promotions are used to encourage potential consumers to try a product and, hopefully, to purchase it again. They may make use of a number of devices.

- ✪ **Free trial samples of a product**

- ✪ **Discount coupons or vouchers**

- ✪ **Cash refund of purchase**

- ✪ **Bargain packs**

- ✪ **Free gifts with the product**

- ✪ **Rewards for loyalty 'such as air miles'**

- ✪ **Point-of-sale displays or demonstrations**

- ✪ **Competitions**

- ✪ **Special deals such as zero per cent finance arrangements**

- ✪ **Loss-leaders (prices cut on particular products to encourage customers into a shop)**

- ✪ **Prizes, bonuses and other inducements to sales forces**

Trade promotions are aimed at distributors to encourage them to stock a particular product. They may involve the use of cash incentives to display and advertise a particular product, special prizes or bonuses paid to organisations prepared to stock the product or service, and exhibitions or product conventions aimed at potential distributors. The panel below gives a list of reasons for sales promotion.

SALES PROMOTION

- ✪ **To introduce a new product**

- ✪ **To encourage consumers to buy larger quantities of existing lines**

- ✪ **To encourage consumers to buy products at off-peak times**

- ✪ **To secure repeat business**

- ✪ **To challenge competitors**

- ✪ **To increase sales**

- ✪ **To regain former customers**

THE SALES PROMOTION CAMPAIGN

For a sales promotion to achieve its objectives it is important to ensure that it keeps within budget and clearly targets the potential group of consumers or distributors. The panel adjacent describes how the *Pepsi Max* 1994 sales promotion achieved its required degree of targeting.

MAXIMISING YOUR MARKET IMPACT

Today's 16-to-24 year-olds are notoriously difficult to reach. Their typical 'seen that, done that' attitude means they tend to be fairly indifferent to both marketing and promotional messages.

On the face of it, trying to persuade this cynical, discerning and street-wise group to participate in something as corny and old-fashioned as product sampling would appear to be a daunting task. Yet, last summer, the UK distributor for PepsiCo, Britvic Soft Drinks, targeted this very age group with a sampling campaign for its new, sugar-free cola, *Pepsi Max* – and managed to convince 470,000 consumers to try the product.

Britvic Soft Drinks managed to spark this level of interest among the 16-to-24 year-old age group by giving them, as it were, a taste of their own medicine. Instead of the traditionally polite 'would-you-like-one-of-these?' approach to sampling, it mounted an intrusive, but good humoured, tasting campaign which tried to mirror the irreverent behaviour and 'street-cred' image of the young characters seen in *Pepsi Max's* popular television commercials.

The characters represent the age group of under-25s that US marketers have dubbed 'Generation X' – a term coined five years ago by the American writer Douglas Coupland. Some observers believe it is the most important development in youth culture since the rise of the teenager in the '50s. This group might be cynical about life, but they are aware of their value and power as consumers – and they are advertising literate.

By the age of 18, most UK teenagers will have seen more than 140,000 TV ads – and their resistance to advertising and promotional campaigns is high. They know the meaning of 'branding' and 'marketing' and are sceptical about the guile of advertisers. At the same time, however, they recognise that advertising is a form of entertainment and they will respond favourably to ads which are fun – although they still won't buy products they don't want. Britvic Soft Drinks has already scored well here – with its wacky, irreverent *Tango* campaign – as has Golden Wonder, with its *Pot Noodles* brand.

So Britvic aimed its high-energy ads – under the banner 'Live Life to the Max' – at this target group. They were designed to overcome the negative images associated with sugar-free diet drinks by highlighting the fast-paced, exciting lifestyles that appeal to young consumers – showing 'hip' young characters taking part in various, high-risk adventure activities. According to PepsiCo, the ads 'overhauled the perception of no-sugar drinks' and gave *Pepsi Max* an 'unparalleled image' in the youth market.

'We needed to prove that *Pepsi Max* was not purely an image-based product,' says Tim Davie, marketing manager for Pepsi UK. 'We wanted to create an understanding that, with its full-bodied cola taste in a no-sugar product, it was a genuine product innovation.'

Davie says they decided to use product sampling to 'underpin' the success of the above-the-line advertising. 'Our research showed that, when people tried it, the level of repeat purchase was excellent,' he says. 'We wanted to convert a great image into repeat purchase by working the theme of the ad into the experience of receiving a free sample.'

Last summer, the sales promotion agency HH&S mounted a 'Max Attack' sampling campaign which visited all the major conurbations in a two-month period. HH&S explained that they designed the national roadshow to 'bring the brand to life on the street'. To do this, they used sampling teams of young actors who looked like, and emulated, the outrageous characters from the *Pepsi Max* commercials. These 'Max Boys' toured the country in distinctive, *Pepsi Max*-branded white Jeeps and irreverently handed out product samples in shopping malls, stores, nightclubs and during special events. 'It was "in your face" sampling to reflect the style of the advertising,' says Paul Vines, joint managing director of HH&S. 'It was intrusive and impactful and, as it was highly-targeted, it did not suffer from any of the negative connotations of traditional sampling,' he says.

'The lookalike characters appealed to the target audience because of their "leading edge" behaviour and image. They also enjoyed a kind of cult following at special events, with people even asking for autographs.'

According to HH&S, the roadshow was seen by 30,000 to 40,000 consumers a day. They even tied the sampling activity to on-air competitions on local radio.

Britvic Soft Drinks claims the sampling initiative played a 'critical part' in boosting *Pepsi Max's* UK sales by 300 per cent in 1994. It now has five per cent of the UK cola market.

From Marketing, 9 March 1995

The 1990s have seen an increase in the number of organisations which have supported sales promotion with television or radio advertising. In 1994, there was an increase of 160 per cent in the number of promotions supported by advertising. They included such household names as Weetabix, Coca-Cola, Esso, Shell and McDonald's. These organisations recognised that advertising helps to attract customers into retail outlets and encourages them to make purchases, while the sales promotional activity has a role in making people feel happy about a brand, thus making the sale promotion a success.

Another growth area in sales promotions has been the use of balloons. Increasingly, they are being used to launch new products, support in-store promotions, provide promotional give-aways and generate publicity. In August 1994, Walt Disney launched one and a half million balloons to support its release of *Aladdin* on video.

DIRECT MARKETING

Direct marketing includes direct selling, direct mail, telemarketing, use of the Internet, leafleting, roadshows, exhibitions and the sponsorship of events. In all cases, it operates through personal channels of communication where the target market is, in effect. a single customer. By approaching customers individually, an active response is required to the sales pitch.

The 1990s have seen an expansion in direct marketing activities, with the volume of sales achieved equivalent to three per cent of gross domestic product.

DIRECT SELLING

This involves selling things face to face. Typically, it takes place when the buyer visits a shop, although it may occur on the doorstep or through 'party plan' selling (home-based selling events). The advantage of direct selling is that the seller is able to respond to questions, identify customers' specific needs, select particular benefits to demonstrate, and can secure an order immediately.

Door-to-door selling is used both for domestic and industrial consumers. In the majority of cases, the sales representative will either deliver the product immediately, from stocks carried in a car or van, or take an order. The sales person may give advice on re-order quantities and display materials, and provide notice of future advertising campaigns. Where a sales representative is dealing with stockists of consumer durables, such as electrical goods, the person may also spend time attending to technical matters and complaints.

For large retail chains many sales representatives sell directly to the head office, which means much of the advice they give concerns issues of quality, packaging, discounts and special promotions. In order to sell to industrial consumers, it is often necessary to have specialist technical knowledge of plant, machinery and computer systems. These types of sales representatives are referred to as technical representatives.

Party plan selling is aimed at groups of domestic buyers who are brought together by a common contact or friend, who is recruited by the seller. The host receives financial or other benefits to organise the party, with sales being carried out by the organisation's personnel.

DIRECT MAIL

Direct mail involves posting information about an organisation's goods and services to actual or potential customers. It provides a highly targeted approach, with the names of customers, identified in terms of various socio-economic and other criteria, compiled in a list which becomes the basis for a **mail shot**. Ultimately, the success of this approach depends on the quality of the mailing list, and in many cases these are obtained from specialist agencies.

The most effective direct mail campaigns tend to be through a letter or promotional communication which is simple and to the point. It has both to stimulate interest and provide a means of response, such as a coupon or postage paid envelope. The response rate may be increased through the use of an inducement such as a prize draw.

The use of direct mail is growing rapidly. It is used by charities, book clubs, travel and leisure companies, financial services companies and political parties. In 1994, over £16m was spent on direct mail, a 12 per cent increase on the previous year's figure. This represents 2.7 billion items delivered (see *Fig 3.19*).

ACTIVITY

Over a period of four weeks, make a collection of the advertising and promotional literature that is posted to your home. Analyse each communication and record the following:

- organisation
- product, service or charity appeal

- ✪ **ease of understanding**
- ✪ **impact**
- ✪ **form of response**
- ✪ **appropriateness of any incentives**

On the basis of your findings, rank the communications in order of effectiveness. Write a brief report justifying your views.

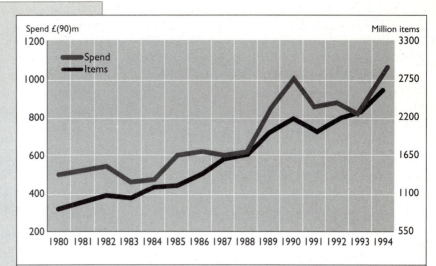

FIGURE 3.19: Direct mail expenditure and number of items delivered 1980-1994
Source: *Marketing*, 6 April 1995

TELEMARKETING

This involves the seller of a product or service communicating with customers directly by telephone. Interested customers may then be visited by a sales representative with a view to completing a sale. This method is used widely in the sale of double glazing, replacement windows, driveways, insurance and financial services. Companies like First Direct and Direct Line insurance have managed to build very successful businesses using this sales method.

The success of telemarketing depends on the ability of the telephone sales staff. A team needs to be properly trained and staff have to be very methodical and well organised (usually, they work to a prepared script).

The use of telemarketing has been encouraged by technological advances such as the development of call centres. These provide a centralised service for receiving and also, increasingly, making telephone calls; a central computer carries out the dialling. The system works through the use of a **target database** of names and numbers. Once the call has been answered, it is routed to a salesperson. If the number dialled is engaged or an answering machine is reached, the call is routed to the back of the queue. The computer can link up with other databases to provide relevant information about the customer, such as the person's address and socio-economic group, enabling the sales person to adapt the sales pitch accordingly.

A similar approach can be taken in receiving calls, for example Abbey National Direct uses software that can recognise the telephone number of a mortgage customer and route the caller to the home loans adviser who dealt with the enquirer previously, thus providing continuity of service.

OTHER DIRECT MARKETING TOOLS

THE INTERNET
The Internet global computer network, or information superhighway, offers new opportunities for advertising and direct selling. In March 1995 there were about 30 million users of the network worldwide with over 500,000 in the United Kingdom. The development of broadband communications is expected to promote interactive use of computers, for example in 'digital shopping'.

LEAFLETING
The door-to-door distribution of leaflets can provide an effective way of targeting a particular area. It is often used by organisations offering domestic services, such as plumbers, electricians, builders, gardeners and painters and decorators. Many voluntary organisations deliver leaflets before making a collection.

ROADSHOWS
As described in the *Pepsi Max* campaign (see above), a roadshow enables a message to be communicated in a series of different locations, where representatives from the organisation can meet potential buyers.

EXHIBITIONS
These may be staffed or unattended. The purpose is to inform potential customers about products or services. One of the most effective is the **trade fair** where a manufacturer may invite a targeted group of distributors and retailers to visit the organisation's stand. Hospitality is sometimes offered

PORTFOLIO ASSIGNMENT

COMMUNICATION CHALLENGE

The class should divide into small groups. Each should select two business organisations currently involved in major campaigns to advertise, publicise and promote their activities. The selection could be from such organisations as a book club, record company, manufacturer of a canned drink, a hotel chain, a credit card company, a chain of fast food outlets, a brewery, or the manufacturer of a chocolate bar.

During a two-week period, the members of the group should monitor and record the advertising, publicity, public relations and promotional activities of the organisations, as the results of this appear in newspapers and magazines, on television and radio and at cinemas and sports, charity and entertainment events. Create a form to record your data.

The group should also find evidence of any direct marketing activities undertaken by the organisations. This may be in the form of a letter which has been sent to a member of the group, their family or a friend. (If this is not available, a request could be made to the organisation for an example.)

Each member of the group should have a set of the record sheets and write a report which compares and contrasts the campaigns and methods of communication used by the organisations.

The report should cover:

✪ the major business activities of the organisations;

✪ their target markets;

✪ the main examples of the use of communications to reach the target markets;

✪ an evaluation of the effectiveness of each communication in terms of awareness raising, securing greater brand loyalty, increasing sales and lengthening the life of the product; and

✪ any efforts to meet the requirements of the Advertising Standards Authority. Also, suggest how a less ethical organisation might have been tempted to abuse the ASA's standards.

Customer satisfaction through sales methods and service

CUSTOMER SATISFACTION AND CUSTOMER SERVICE

The ultimate marketing objective is to make the sale, but in doing so it is important to achieve the highest possible level of customer satisfaction as this will lead to repeat sales, recommendations to other potential customers and still further sales.

Achieving customer satisfaction requires an organisation to have a **culture** which emphasises customer service. This means that all employees must have the same values, beliefs and ways of communicating which reflect the needs of the customer. Employees must be trained to have an appropriate open-mindedness and readiness to act in response to customers' needs. They must strive to achieve quality in their own work and be willing to go out of their way to deliver that same level of quality to customers. This culture, of putting the customer first, must be handed down from the top of the organisation.

Organisations, such as Marks and Spencer, have built their reputation on providing a very high standard of customer service. The staff are trained to accept the principle that the customer is always right and that their wishes can be gauged by looking at purchases on the shop floor. Similarly, when Mercury Communications was created, in 1982, it provided a guide to its services which stated that: 'Mercury was created to provide the most competitive service possible at lower costs, placing the needs of the customer first.'

ACTIVITY

List four organisations which you consider to have a culture of customer service.

In each case, identify the means by which the organisation attempts to increase consumer satisfaction and how the employees contribute towards this.

Suggest how the organisations benefit commercially by operating in this way.

Organisations involved in developing a culture of customer service have to do this at both a **strategic** and **operational** level. Strategically, it is necessary to evaluate the customers' wants and then to design a package of services which meets their expectations. For example, customers will have certain expectations when they enter a dry cleaner's. These must be realised in terms of the standards of the counter staff, the availability of advice, the quality of the cleaning, the treatment of the items of clothing in terms of hangers and covers, the accuracy of the bill, the methods of payment, the atmosphere of the shop and the competitiveness of the price.

Operationally, any service must be well delivered with consistent standards in terms of each customer visit, different geographical locations and individual employees. For example, an organisation like McDonald's strives to maintain the same high standards of cleanliness, speed and quality of service and food whether the outlet is in London, Paris or Moscow.

Increasingly, those organisations which are committed to achieving the highest possible levels of customer satisfaction recognise that this is only possible if everyone in the organisation seeks to do their job as well as they can for the people they serve. This wider view of what is meant by a 'customer' goes beyond the **external customer**, who actually buys or uses the product or receives the service, to one which includes anyone for whom an employee within the organisation provides a service, or who has need of what is supplied. This allows for the idea of the **internal customer** – those who work in the same organisation, who have the same external customers and share the same organisational goals, and whose work is in some way dependent on that done by the employee or by others in the organisation. Consequently, the service that an employee provides internally to fellow employees has a direct impact on the quality of the service delivered to the external customer.

In order to achieve a high level of quality employees have to think in a particular way: they have to recognise that what to them may be a routine duty may be of crucial significance for the effective performance of the internal customers that they serve. Under these circumstances, all employees need to know not only what they have to do and how to do it, but also why they are doing it and what the result will be for their colleagues if something is not done correctly and to the appropriate standard.

The commercial advantages of achieving high standards of customer service have become increasingly recognised by organisations in the 1990s. In many cases, customer service has been adopted by major business organisations as a strategic objective. These organisations have recognised that it brings the following benefits:

- ⊗ **Organisations that differentiate their goods and services on the basis of service can ask higher prices for comparative products or services and achieve higher profit margins.**

- ⊗ **Good customer service is often associated with greater customer loyalty, which makes an organisation less open to attack by 'clone' competitors and ensures that it will not be as adversely affected by an economic downturn as others may be.**

- ⊗ **Due to the premium placed on customer service, organisations are likely to experience more of the benefits associated with a period of economic boom.**

- ⊗ **Having a reputation for high–quality customer service often means that the business does not need to spend as much on advertising.**

- ⊗ **A business which develops a culture of customer service and recognises the existence of internal customers is likely to have a more contented workforce, with lower absenteeism and higher employee retention rates.**

DIRECT AND INDIRECT SALES METHODS

In deciding upon the suitability of different sales methods, it is important to consider the strategic objectives of the organisation and the required culture of customer service and satisfaction. Basically, a decision has to be made as to whether an organisation should directly sell its own products or services or use an indirect selling method, working through an appropriate intermediary within the channel of distribution.

DIRECT SALES METHODS

These involve direct contact taking place only between the producer and the customer. Such methods are part of a direct marketing strategy as described previously. They include the following:

- ⊗ **television and radio advertising featuring ordering information and, often, exclusive access to the product (music compilations on compact disc);**

- ⊗ **door-to-door selling, both to domestic and industrial consumers (cleaning products);**

- ⊗ **telephone selling, involving an initial contact followed up with a visit from a sales representative (double glazing);**

- ⊗ **selling directly from factory premises (pine bookcases, bedroom furniture);**

- ⊗ **selling through a mail order catalogue (holidays); and**

- ⊗ **pyramid selling, which is a form of multi-level marketing involving a 'pyramid' of sales persons, with a few initial members recruiting others who, in turn, recruit still more, creating an expanding chain of sales people (cosmetics).**

All of these methods have the advantage for manufacturers of allowing them greater control over the marketing and selling of their products. However, the 'downside' can be that they involve the manufacturer in an expensive storage and distribution operation.

ACTIVITY

Mail order advertisements can often be seen in newspapers and magazines. Where the company selling the goods has been able to by-pass both the wholesaler and the retailer, it may be able to offer the goods at attractive prices.

Cut out a large mail order advertisement from a magazine.

Explain why the company may have decided to use this direct form of selling.

How are both the company and the consumer likely to benefit?

Explain why the product is advertised in the particular magazine.

Do you feel that the content and style of the advert would be likely to sell the product?

How else might the product have been sold?

INDIRECT SALES METHODS

These involve manufacturers working through a third party or intermediary in order to sell their products. These intermediaries are part of the distribution channel, which traditionally has three stages of operation:

- ❂ **Manufacturing – making the product;**

- ❂ **Wholesaling – the holding of large stocks and breaking bulk into retail packs; and**

- ❂ **Retailing – the sale of the product to the final buyer, or consumer.**

The decision by a manufacturer to hand over the **wholesaling** and retailing activity to an intermediary is based on organisational, operational and financial considerations.

The wholesaler provides a number of benefits to the manufacturer.

1 Wholesalers buy products in relatively large quantities from the manufacturer, which they stock and then break down the bulk, selling on in smaller quantities to retailers. This allows the manufacturer to benefit from fewer but larger orders, with resulting economies of scale for longer production runs and the avoidance of what may be a high minimum outlay for storage, sales and transport facilities.

2 The manufacturer avoids having to cover the delivery costs associated with small consignments to a large number of widely dispersed retail outlets.

3 Independent wholesalers may operate a single warehouse or a chain of warehouses giving wider regional coverage and, in many cases, national distribution.

4 Specialist wholesalers may concentrate on such things as beer, wines and spirits, fruit and vegetables, meat, fish, footwear, clothing, sports equipment, carpets, china and glassware, hardware, electrical goods, books, and furniture. These specialist wholesalers are very important for goods where the demand is very high at certain times of the year. The wholesaler that deals in swimsuits, for example, will place orders for them during the winter and build up stocks in the warehouse well before the summer months. The manufacturer of swimsuits can therefore keep the factory going at a steady rate during the whole of the year. This will help the manufacturer to run the business more efficiently. The wholesaler will also have enough swimsuits in stock to meet the very large increase in demand during the summer months. Without the wholesaler, manufacturers of swimsuits would find it very difficult to meet demand, and there would be a shortage.

5 The wholesaler may undertake specialist activities involving blending, processing or packaging, which when conducted on behalf of many producers can be carried out on a more economic scale. These specialist skills are of particular value when dealing with commodities such as tea, coffee and wool.

6 In the case of perishable products such as fruit and vegetables, the specialist wholesaler should be able to distribute the products more rapidly to a scattered market. Consider, for example, the role of the great London markets including Covent Garden (flowers, fruit and vegetables), Billingsgate (fish) and Smithfield (meat).

7 A new manufacturer with very limited trading experience and financial resources may initially use a wholesaler who will have a greater knowledge of local customers in terms of credit-worthiness and the size and frequency of orders. They can also pass on advice to the retailer regarding shelf, counter and window displays.

8 Wholesale merchants act as a link between manufacturers and the firms that need raw materials, parts, equipment and machinery. This is known as selling to the trade and could involve builders, plumbers, decorators and timber merchants. Merchants are also willing to build up their stocks in warehouses or yards with those items which are in seasonal demand. This is the case, for example, with building materials, as less building and decorating work goes on in the winter months as compared to other times of the year.

It may be concluded that selling through a wholesaler confers benefits on both the manufacturer and retailer. However, some criticisms are levelled at the wholesale function on the grounds that the wholesaler simply takes a cut and contributes to higher prices. This can mean that if either the manufacturer or retailer believes that it can perform the wholesaler's services, it will seek to do so in the interests both of profit and competitive sales. In fact, the development of large supermarket and DIY chains has meant that, in many cases, the wholesaling function of stocking and breaking bulk has become increasingly integrated with the retail function, with retailers taking advantage of price discounts associated with bulk buying.

Some products by their very nature are distributed directly by manufacturers to **retailers**. These include relatively expensive products where distribution costs can be borne by the manufacturer without a severe impact upon the competitive position or profit margins. It is not necessary for retailers to deal in large and varied stocks of consumer durables; they are not expected to buy television sets or washing-machines in bulk. Manufacturers may perhaps conduct their own wholesaling function in such products where after-sales service is required, and where close contact with retail units providing such services will be necessary.

The increased mobility of consumers has increased the popularity for manufacturers of dealing directly with retailers. This has increased the turnover of fewer but larger retail units. Where congestion in city centres has created problems, retail units have responded by taking sites in out-of-town shopping centres and by establishing hypermarkets. This also assists in deliveries and increases warehousing facilities. Manufacturers have benefited from the creation of new motorways and the development of larger commercial vehicles, which have reduced costs and improved the efficiency of their distribution system.

Some wholesalers have responded positively to these developments by offering cash and carry warehouse facilities, where retailers can choose from large displays of goods. Retailers pay for the goods before leaving and use their own vehicles to take them away. This allows the wholesaler to offer lower prices, as they save some of the costs associated with paperwork, sales representatives and delivery service. Cash and carry services may be used by people who hold a special card that allows them to buy at wholesale prices. These cards may also be issued to other businesses, such as hotels, restaurants and sports and social clubs.

The retailer operates a business which stocks a particular type of product, such as a clothes shop, or an extensive range of products, such as a department store, for making sales to consumers. In so doing, retailers have traditionally provided a convenient point of sale, at the end of the distribution channel, for manufacturers' products.

However, the relationship between retailers and manufacturers is changing. The development of supermarket and DIY chains has meant that many retailers have become much more demanding in their dealings with manufacturers. Retailers have been able to use their bulk buying power to obtain substantial price discounts from manufacturers and, in the case of larger retail groups, retailers have established an extensive own-label brand business in direct competition with manufacturers' brands. By providing retailers with the increased opportunity to use price as a competitive weapon within the marketing mix, consumers have benefited.

Agents and distributors sometimes feature within the distribution channel as another type of intermediary. The major purpose of using an agent is to generate new business contracts. In many cases, a manufacturer will employ an agent to obtain new wholesale customers, or a wholesaler will use an agent when seeking to establish new retail accounts.

Distributors are more independent than agents. They usually buy from the manufacturer at a discount and resell with a 'mark up'. In many cases a distributor will demand an exclusive sales arrangement, whereby it alone may sell the manufacturer's product in a certain area. The advantage to the manufacturer of going through a distributor is that it can offer access to additional sales outlets in new areas.

Agents and distributors are of particular value to companies wishing to establish a presence in foreign markets. The company could either sell through an export agency in the UK or appoint an agent or distributor in the country abroad. In the case of the latter, a suitable appointment could mean not only that the business sells its product abroad, but it also receives useful information in relation to factors such as developments in the market, suitable promotions and the need for product modification and updating. In many cases, the agent or distributor may also supply the after-sales service on which customers will judge the reliability of the business.

THE ROLE AND RESPONSIBILITY OF THE SALESPERSON

Selling is the part of the marketing process concerned with maintaining or increasing demand by overcoming consumer resistance or inertia. The salesperson attempts to do this by presenting the product or communicating persuasive messages to the potential client. This may be carried out at each stage of the channel of distribution, from the manufacturer to the wholesaler, the wholesaler to the retailer, and the retailer to the consumer.

Selling is unlike other aspects of marketing in that it depends entirely upon human relationships, i.e. contact between the salesperson and the customer. Consequently, the skills associated with successful selling are essentially people-oriented, including good communication, interpersonal skills and negotiating abilities.

Jobs in selling may involve working as part of a sales force, making personal or telephone contact with industrial and commercial buyers in factories, shops, local authorities, utilities, service industries and charities, or selling directly to individuals and members of households in shops and retail outlets.

STAGES IN THE SELLING PROCESS

MAKING CONTACT WITH CUSTOMERS

Sales staff provide the major link between the organisation and the customer. They must be capable of knowing how and where to make contact with existing or potential customers. For example, selling engineering components will involve building up a relationship with the purchasing departments of various engineering companies. This may be achieved by keeping the customer up to date with changes in technical specifications or design features through visits and telephone calls. In any personal dealings with existing customers, and in particular new customers, the salesperson must generate confidence by appearing honest, knowledgeable, business-like and professional, but should also be approachable, sociable and friendly.

In the case of a salesperson in a retail outlet, there is less time to establish a relationship with the customer, so first impressions are important. Sales staff should be neat and tidy, have a personality which helps them to strike up a good relationship with customers and to be able to engage their interest in a product. Customers should also be made

to feel at ease and believe that the salesperson is taking a genuine interest in them and is acting in their best interest.

IDENTIFYING THE CUSTOMER'S NEEDS

By careful questioning and observation, the salesperson should be able to develop a knowledge of customers' circumstances and establish their real needs. This should then be taken into account when presenting a product or service to the customer.

PRESENTING AND DEMONSTRATING THE PRODUCT OR SERVICE

The salesperson should target those products or services which particularly meet the needs of the customer. Every effort should be made to stress the benefits of the product or service in terms of what the salesperson's organisation can offer and how this compares with the competition. In doing this, the salesperson must be able to draw on extensive **product knowledge** and reference should be made to satisfied customers who could vouch for the reliability of the product. The main features of the product or service should be demonstrated, and, ideally, the potential buyer should be allowed to try out the product.

If any queries are raised during the demonstration these should be viewed in a positive way, as they mean that the potential customer is expressing an interest. The salesperson should always listen very carefully to the customer's reservations and, if necessary, put forward in a calm manner an alternative point of view. Wherever possible, the salesperson should take the opportunity to reiterate the benefits, reliability and features of the product or service.

NEGOTIATING THE PRICE AND CONDITIONS OF SALE

Negotiation involves the salesperson and potential customer conferring in order to find a compromise on price or reach agreement on some aspect of the conditions of sale. Sales staff can only be effective in doing this if they have been properly briefed and have clear objectives to meet. This will allow them to make concessions and, where necessary, to move away from their original position.

Any negotiation involves both parties in making a series of theoretical proposals which are then adjusted in order to arrive at a compromise solution which should as near as possible satisfy both parties. The art of negotiation is to be firm but fair and not to become too aggressive.

Obviously, the extent to which it is appropriate to negotiate will depend upon the type of product or service, its relative price and the complexity of the conditions of sale. For example, there is very little scope to negotiate when conducting the sale of a chocolate bar, but far more when selling a car or a computerised production control system.

CLOSING THE SALE

Once all negotiations have been concluded, and an agreement has been reached, the salesperson should judge the moment to close the sale and secure a firm commitment for an order. There are a number of devices which may be used to bring this about. The salesperson may summarise the position and ask for the order, or offer a final concession to clinch the immediate sale, or assume the buyer wants the product and finalise the conditions of the sale.

AFTER-SALES SERVICE

This covers all the back-up services and facilities provided by the supplier to the customer. It may include free maintenance and repairs, a telephone service to deal with customers' queries and an express parts delivery service. The provision of these services helps to enhance customer loyalty and provides valuable feedback about goods and services.

ACTIVITY

SITUATION

Paul Green works as a sales assistant for Holmes and Sutcliffe, a department store belonging to the House of Lothian retail group. He joined the store after completing a GNVQ in Business and has just completed a 18-month training course. This involved working in a variety of store departments, as well as other areas such as the warehouse and display.

After the training period his first appointment has been as a sales assistant in the china and glassware department. Although he is not involved in selling highly technical items, he has quickly learned that a high degree of product knowledge is required. He needs to know what determines the quality of glass and china, the various uses of the different kinds of glasses and other items, how they should be handled and displayed; and he must be able to recognise the various traditional designs and be able to talk about their various manufacturers. In order to build up and extend his product knowledge, he spends a great deal of time studying the suppliers' catalogues and brochures.

Paul has always got on well with all kinds of people and he has a friendly personality which puts customers at their ease and makes them feel that they can trust his advice and judgement. He has a good sense of humour and is always cheerful, but manages to strike the all-important balance between being friendly to customers and giving them the respect they require.

During his training the need to be polite and well-mannered was always stressed, and his experience on the sales floor has made him realise that such an approach pays dividends. Customers usually respond to a friendly approach, and even some of the awkward customers become more reasonable when they are treated courteously and with tact and patience. This helps to create a pleasant atmosphere on the sales floor and improves Paul's job satisfaction, as well as his sales commission!

Paul is learning how to spot different types of customers and to alter his approach when necessary. For example, when a smartly dressed gentleman insisted on buying what he claimed were sherry glasses, which were in fact liqueur glasses, Paul had the delicate job of explaining that the customer was mistaken. Other 'problem' customers are parents who allow their children to run riot in the store, picking up valuable items on display and knocking into the display stands. Here, the problem is one of knowing how to complete a sale with the customer, while tactfully pointing out that the children are becoming a nuisance. Paul can also recognise the type of customer who wants to be served quickly, efficiently and with the minimum of conversation.

When he first joined the store, Paul was immediately impressed by the style and image of the assistant manager in the furniture department. In particular, he noticed that his method of speech was always clear and concise and that the way he expressed himself enabled him to 'get through' to the customer. He didn't have a 'posh' voice but was well-spoken. Paul realised that he had some faults in his own speech; he tended to be a bit hesitant and his choice of words was rather limited. As a result, he has worked hard to improve his speech and to widen his vocabulary by reading brochures and leaflets.

The store manager still feels that there are a couple of areas to which Paul should pay more attention. Although he tries to be neat and tidy, half way through the day his clothes tend to be rather crumpled and creased. This is exacerbated by his tendency to slouch a little and lean against the counter. His personal hygiene is fine, but there have been times when his hair has been a bit too 'fashionable' for the image of the store.

TASKS

The situation described above highlights many of the qualities that help to make a successful salesperson in a department store.

The class should divide into groups of four and one member of each group should volunteer to be assessed by the others as to the qualities in the form below. Each of the assessors should have a copy of the list and give marks. The results should then be averaged to give an overall mark out of 54 (the maximum possible).

The roles may be changed, until all members of the class have been assessed by a panel of three. The top three salespeople in the class should be identified.

	MARK
Dress and general appearance	
Personal grooming - hair and nails	
Posture and general bearing	
Oral skills and method of speech	
Politeness and manners	
Friendliness towards other people	
Cheerfulness	
Ability to adapt to other people	
Ability and willingness to investigate and learn about things	
TOTAL	

MARKING SYSTEM

Excellent	6
Very good	5
Good	4
Average	3
Acceptable	2
Below average	1
Poor	0

THE SALESPERSON AND THE LAW

There are several laws which seek to protect customers in their dealings with salespeople. Those involved in selling must make sure that they are aware of the implications of this legislation for their work.

TRADE DESCRIPTIONS ACTS 1968 AND 1972

The 1968 Act makes it illegal to give a false description of a good. This covers descriptions in writing, in advertisements or in anything which the seller says when discussing the good with a customer. The Act also covers the way in which goods are priced. The seller cannot charge a higher price than the one marked on the good. It is also illegal to claim that the price of a good has been reduced unless the same good was previously offered at the higher price for a period of at least 28 days in the last six months.

The 1972 Act makes it illegal to sell goods that have been manufactured abroad by trying to give the customer the impression that the goods were made in the UK.

UNSOLICITED GOODS AND SERVICES ACTS 1971 AND 1975

These were designed to control what is known as 'inertia selling', i.e. sending unsuspecting people goods through the post which they hadn't ordered and relying on their ignorance or apathy to extract payment. Fines can be imposed on those businesses making demands for payment for goods and services which are unsolicited.

The Acts provide that any unsolicited goods may be kept by the recipient without payment after a period of 30 days provided that the recipient gives notice to the sender asking that the goods be collected. Alternatively, the recipient can do nothing, that is give no notice to the seller, and the goods become the recipient's as an unconditional gift after six months.

PRICES ACT 1974

This covers the ways in which a shop must show its prices. All food and drink must carry a price. In the case of pre-packed food, such as meat and cheese, the pack must also indicate the price per lb (weight). Food such as fruit and vegetables sold over a counter or on a self-selection basis in a supermarket must also have their prices clearly displayed.

CONSUMER CREDIT ACT 1974

This regulates the way in which a business may offer credit facilities to its consumers (or debtors). The main points that would have to be allowed for in a business proposal are as follows:

- ⊗ **Every credit agency must obtain a licence from the director-general of the Office of Fair Trading.**

- ⊗ **There is control over advertisements for credit which may be misinterpreted, i.e. they are misleading.**

- ⊗ **The credit agreement must be properly drawn up and contain terms laid down in regulations by the government, for example in relation to the debtor's principal rights and duties.**

- ⊗ **The credit arrangement must show the annual percentage rate at which interest will be charged.**

- ⊗ **The debtor is entitled to a copy of the agreement at the time of the contract, and a second copy within seven days if the agreement is accepted at a later date.**

SALE OF GOODS ACT 1979, AS EXTENDED BY SUPPLY OF GOODS AND SERVICES ACT 1982

This indicates clearly the responsibility of any business in selling goods and services. A legal contract exists between the buyer and seller of a good or service. Once the offer to buy a good has been accepted then the seller and not the manufacturer has to deal with any complaint. The 1982 Act lays down three basic conditions regarding the quality of goods and services that a business may sell.

- ⊗ **Goods must be of merchantable quality: they must be reasonably fit for their normal purpose. A new item must not be broken or damaged and must work correctly. If a good is very cheap, however, then the customer must generally expect less quality than a more expensive version of the same good.**

- ⊗ **Goods must be as described. This covers the wording on the package, display signs and oral statements by the trader.**

- ⊗ **Goods must be fit for any particular intended purpose. Apart from being fit for their normal purpose, a trader may assure the customer that the good is** **also suitable for another use. For example, a customer may ask if a paint can also be used on plastic guttering. If the trader says that it would be suitable, the buyer can claim recompense if it proves otherwise.**

A business cannot attempt to remove any of these rights by getting customers to sign a guarantee which offers less protection than is already available under the law.

FOOD ACT 1984

This lays down regulations governing the production, distribution and sale of food, which are enforced by local authority environmental health officers. Criminal prosecution may occur where, for example, food or drink is being sold which is felt to be unfit for human consumption, or the contents of any food have been wrongly described, or claims have been made about the nutritional value of food which are misleading.

WEIGHTS AND MEASURES ACT 1985

This provides detailed rules regarding the weighing and measurement of goods. For example, in the case of prepacked meat or cheese the weight must be accurately marked on the packet. Breaches of the rules can result in prosecution.

CONSUMER PROTECTION ACT 1987

This makes it a criminal offence to supply any consumer goods which do not meet with general safety requirements. Businesses have a general duty to trade safely and to meet certain standards regarding furniture and fire hazards and such products as electrical appliances, toys and babies' dummies.

ACTIVITY

Each student should select a product which they can easily bring into school or college. Efforts should be made to choose the kind of product where a customer is likely to want the help and advice of a salesperson if they are thinking of buying it. The kinds of products that can be used for this task are listed below:

pair of shoes	electric drill
crash helmet	calculator
sports bag	hair dryer
radio	pullover
attache case	road atlas
jeans	kettle
iron	an item of sportswear
toaster	shaver
fountain pen	glue
anorak	

Determine how much the product would cost if bought today and identify all those features of the product which might be brought to the attention of a potential customer by a salesperson in the kind of shop where it is sold.

Assume the role of a salesperson and present your product to the group. At the end of each presentation the rest of the group should give their opinion on the performance and, in particular, highlight anything that might tend to mislead a customer or could potentially be in breach of the law.

MANAGEMENT AND ADMINISTRATION OF THE SALES FUNCTION

The contribution of the sales function in marketing is to help to generate the volume of sales required to yield the planned profit. In certain cases, however, this may be defined as maximising sales of particular items, increasing sales abroad or providing market research information. To achieve this, those involved in sales must pay special attention to ensuring the effective operation of the sales force and the efficient administration of the sales office. Retail selling has similar objectives, with the same need to achieve high standards of management and administration.

ORGANISING THE SALES FORCE

The sales manager has to take responsibility for organising the direct sales force which works exclusively for the organisation. This may be divided into the internal salespeople who conduct business from the organisation's premises, either personally or on the telephone, together with the field sales force which travels to visit customers. In certain cases, the sales manager will also take responsibility for the sales agents, dealers or brokers who are employed on a contractual basis and paid entirely on commission.

The **direct sales force** may be organised into territories according geographical area, product or market segment. The allocation of territories may entail sales targets.

The performance of the salesperson may be measured in a number of ways, including in terms of the following:

- **orders secured per visit;**
- **sales revenue generated against the number of calls;**
- **the ratio of profit to calls;**
- **the ratio of orders per call; and**
- **the average value of an order.**

Obviously, if such criteria are to be applied, the allocation of territories should take account of travel time and expense, equality of sales opportunity and, hence, potential earnings.

MOTIVATING THE SALESFORCE

In order to meet the required level of sales, management must ensure that suitable people have been recruited into the salesforce and that they have received adequate training and induction into the principles of selling and customer service, as well as the organisation's product or services and its administrative procedures.

The salesforce may then be motivated to meet or exceed sales targets by:

- **setting personal, monthly and yearly sales targets based on the projected sales forecasts;**

- **paying the salesforce a basic salary, together with an incentive or commission payment, based on sales achieved;**

- **raising the status of the salesforce by giving its members appropriate job titles, expense allowances and cars;**

- **generating competition between sales personnel through bonuses and rewards for meeting or exceeding sales targets; and**

- **improving communications by sending out sales bulletins, newsletters or memoranda to keep the salesforce up to date with what is happening in the organisation, its successes, new product developments and the actions of its competitors.**

Field selling can be a relatively lonely job, therefore it is important for the sales manager to develop a team approach by being in regular contact with members of the salesforce. This can be done more formally through holding weekly or monthly sales meetings and conferences in order to:

- **keep the salesforce informed about the latest company developments;**

- **introduce new products or modifications to existing ones;**

- **develop strategies to deal with competitors;**

- **introduce new credit control systems or pricing strategies; and**

- **motivate the salesforce.**

Sales conferences are often held on an annual basis and tend to be more formal than sales meetings. In many cases, the owners of the organisation or the directors may attend. Conferences are normally held in order to:

- **achieve a wider understanding of the organisation and its products or services (to this end, design, research and development, and production staff may be invited to attend);**

- **carry out training concerning new products;**

- **review the existing product range and decide whether any modifications are necessary;**

- **review competitors' products and decide on a policy to counteract developments in the market;**

- **focus on successful sales methods; and**

- **bring the internal sales staff into contact with the field salespeople.**

ADMINISTERING THE SALES FUNCTION

The smooth and efficient operation of the sales office is vital if sales targets are to be met and a high standard of customer service achieved. The **sales office** provides several vital services.

1. It acts as a liaison between the customers and the business, which includes dealing with all incoming enquiries, making appointments and handling complaints.

2. It processes orders, which involves receiving the incoming order and checking the accuracy of price, detail and delivery; entering the order onto the manual or computerised system; passing the order to production or purchasing; and passing the completed order to the warehouse for despatch.

3. It maintains records relating to the performance of each salesperson covering: areas worked in, sales achieved, salary, bonuses received and expenses paid.

4. It receives reports from the salesforce regarding the number of calls made, the time taken, stages of negotiations, particular problems, prospecting activities for new customers and the actions of competitors.

5 It maintains records relating to existing, former and new customers. These include a list of major contracts, orders taken, discounts given, special requirements and credit rating.

6 It runs a credit control and rating system, which involves establishing a credit rating for each new customer based on the salesperson's report, trade references, and special enquiries from trade protection societies.

RUNNING A SALES CAMPAIGN

The success of any sales campaign depends upon the efficient operation of the management and administration of the sales function. The campaign has to be developed as part of the overall marketing plan which, in turn, must be tied into the organisation's overall strategic plan. Obviously, a sales campaign will only be successful if it is an integral part of the marketing mix and is coordinated with the activities of purchasing, personnel, production, finance and distribution.

The sales campaign will be targeted in accordance with the findings of market research and supported by various promotional activities, to stimulate interest in the product or service and, ultimately, to achieve higher levels of sales.

The campaign may be promoted to the salesforce, wholesaler and retailer. Letters, memoranda and bulletins may be sent out stating where the effort should be made, how it should be coordinated with the promotion, the features of the product that need to be stressed and the benefits it provides. In many cases the campaign may be accompanied by special incentives for those who manage to achieve a certain (target) level of sales. The launch of the campaign would normally be supported by either a full sales conference or a sales meeting. This would provide the opportunity to help the salesforce to develop the necessary product knowledge, appreciate the unique selling points of the product, and to understand the selling methods and promotional activities that are to be used to support the campaign.

DAEWOO PRONOUNCES DEATH OF THE SALESMAN

The puns and piped music were excruciating. But everything else about Daewoo's much-heralded 'revolutionary approach to car retailing' felt like a gale of fresh air blowing through the motor trade. Here was a car browsing environment with the hassle factor removed and without a salesman in sight.

Research carried out by Daewoo in preparation for its British launch proved a telling indictment of how traditional motor dealers fail to make customers feel welcome. Of the motorists surveyed, 63 per cent said they found showrooms intimidating, a similar percentage reckoned the salesman usually wins, and 86 per cent said they would be prepared to travel up to 50 miles for a better buying experience.

It encouraged Daewoo to dispense with plans for a dealer network and echo instead the growing trend in car insurance by setting up a direct marketing arrangement. By cutting out the middleman, it has achieved keen pricing, bolstered by an unrivalled 'on-the-road' package.

Salesmen on commission are anathema to the formula. Showroom staff, who are not allowed to approach unless invited, earn bonuses based on customer approval of how well they are treated, not how much they spend. But interestingly, each showroom has a 'greeter' to welcome anyone who enters and advise them of the facilities available.

Patrick Farrell, ex-Rover and Daewoo's marketing director, said that pre-launch studies revealed that many prospective buyers are inhibited by the atmosphere of traditional showrooms and feel more at ease by being welcomed in and 'given permission' to explore what is on offer.

The price of every Daewoo includes delivery to your home, tax for the first year, number plates, a full tank of petrol, a three-year/60,000 miles warranty, three years' membership of the AA including European cover, and free servicing for the first three years. It can also be returned for a refund or exchange any time in the first month. There is a free mobile phone if you want it, and when the car needs servicing, Daewoo promises to collect and return it from and to your home or work, and lend you another car while yours is in the garage. The first 1,000 sold also come with the extraordinary pledge of a free replacement car when the new registration arrives on 1 August.

Eschewing a dealer network, Daewoo has organised servicing through the Halfords garage chain, but with its own staff on hand to ensure that customers are well looked after. The arrangement also provides a useful way of reaching potential buyers. In future, when another make of car goes to a Halfords garage for its MOT or a service, a leaflet left on the driving seat will woo the owner with the attractions of a new Daewoo.

One of the cleverest aspects of the Daewoo set-up is the way the whole family is catered for and coaxed into the buying experience. Unusually, a Daewoo showroom's aisles are wide enough to steer a double-buggy around without the usual anxiety about scratching a car, and the flooring is soft, enabling a woman in high-heeled shoes to walk around without clicking conspicuously. These may seem trivial points, but they resolve two aspects that alienate women from dealer showrooms.

While a parent explores the Daewoo range on an interactive CD-ROM touch-screen display, bored children can be kept amused in a supervised crèche, where they have their own touch-screen computer.

The adult version lets you choose a model on the screen, view it in different colours, decide on any extras, see the price, check the cost of insuring it, work out monthly payments on a finance deal, and print out all the relevant information to take home. The child version lets users design their own car and gives them a personalised sketch of it to take home.

From *The Observer*, 9 April 1995

ACTIVITY

⊗ **Read the newspaper article relating to Daewoo (see panel).**

⊗ **Discuss in small groups whether such an approach really represents the 'death of the salesman'.**

⊗ **Decide whether customers are likely to welcome such an approach.**

⊗ **Identify any potential legal problems that might be associated with selling in this way.**

PORTFOLIO ASSIGNMENT

SELLING METHODS

As a school or college group, contact a sales manager from a local company. Invite the manager to give a short presentation on a recent sales campaign and to explain the methods used.

Ask the manager to supply, wherever possible, copies of the following:

✪ in-house literature describing the company's activities and product range;

✪ the company's mission statement;

✪ documents relating to the ordering process;

✪ reports of promotional activities and literature used to support the sales campaign;

✪ a job description and specification for a salesperson; and

✪ minutes of relevant sales conferences and meetings.

As a group, prepare questions for the sales manager on:

✪ sales methods;

✪ methods of distribution;

✪ incentives offered to the sales force, wholesalers and retailers;

✪ any legal problems encountered; and

✪ policy towards customer service.

(Different members of the group should be assigned to ask the questions.)

On an individual basis, write a report which critically appraises the sales methods used by the company, how it manages and administers the sales function, any problems it experiences in operating within the law and the level of customer service it is able to achieve.

MULTIPLE CHOICE QUESTIONS

In each case circle the correct response (there is only one).

1 Which aspect of the marketing mix is most concerned with revenue?

A product

B price

C promotion

D place

2 Market segmentation is necessary because:

A business organisations can satisfy all consumers equally in a given market

B customers with similar characteristics behave inconsistently

C different strategies need to be used for different sets of customers

D the market should always be viewed as a totality

3 The value of branding is that it may do all of the following except:

A differentiate a product from the competition

B establish consumer loyalty and make demand more price elastic

C convey a feeling of quality and reliability

D help to define and identify a product clearly

4 Which of the following is not a benefit associated with packaging?

A it helps to differentiate the product

B it helps to draw attention to the product

C it adds value to the product

D it reduces the price of the product

5 In terms of the product lifecycle which of the following statements is false?

A the development stage requires heavy expenditure on market research

B products usually become established in the market very quickly

C to sustain growth promotional activities will be focused on building consumer commitment and loyalty

D the maturity stage may be extended by moving the product into another market segment

6 Target profit pricing is when:

A an organization charges the same as competitors

B higher prices are charged in line with customer perceptions of the product

C a standard mark up is added to total costs

D break-even analysis is used to illustrate total costs and revenues at different levels of sales

7 Market research is necessary because among other factors:

✪ social changes influence the choice of distributive outlets used by consumers

✪ an organisation's sales will be affected by changes in other markets and in the economy as a whole

✪ advertising is an important source of employment and promotes the growth of independent advertising agencies

A all of the above

B the first two only

C the second two only

D the first

8 Which of the following is not a form of secondary research?

A analysing a business organisation's sales records

B conducting a postal survey of householders

C monitoring economic trends through the business media

D studying the demographic trends shown in *Social Trends*

9 Test marketing may cover all of the following except:

A the method of production

B the distribution system

C the sales organisation

D the product

10 Accurate sampling requires all of the following except:

A the sample should reproduce the characteristics of the 'universe'

B the sample should replicate the same proportion of people with certain characteristics as in the sub-groups

C the size of the sample should reflect the number of sub-groups

D there should be a smaller sample for a less uniform 'universe'

11 The responses to a questionnaire are likely to be biased under the following circumstances:

A the questions are highly structured

B the questions are open-ended

C the questions are in two parts or stages

D the questions are unambiguous

12 When conducting a market survey personal interviews are employed because:

A they are generally less expensive than other methods

B interviewers are always free of bias

C the interviewers will never vary their approach

D they achieve the greatest response

13 Which of the following statements is false?

A the launch of a new brand of coffee is likely to be undertaken through impersonal types of communication

B an element of personal communication is likely to be associated with the sale of timeshare apartments in Spain

C advertising involves personal forms of communication aimed at stressing the unique selling points of a product

D it is generally advisable to advertise mail order items at the weekend

14 The successful targeting of a communication to a particular market segment may be complicated by all of the following, except :

A the difficulty of obtaining feedback

B the actions of opinion leaders

C consumer advice provided by government agencies

D conducting extensive research into the characteristics of the targeted consumers making up the market segment

15 The use of television as a means of targeting the market accurately has been made more difficult by all of the following, except :

A rival channels scheduling popular game shows or soap operas at the same time

B the growth of cable television

C the wider ownership of video recorders

D the increasing number of households owning more than one television set

16 The Advertising Standards Authority takes responsibility for all of the following, except :

A administering a code of practice for all non-broadcast media

B providing guidance to advertisers as to the acceptability of particular adverts

C dealing with complaints from the general public on the standards of advertisements

D taking direct legal action against untruthful, misleading or offensive advertisements

17 Which of the following statements is (or are) true about public relations?

⊗ **it is a means of promoting and publicising a business's company image**

⊗ **a PR campaign may be preceded by a SWOT analysis**

⊗ **it may involve the use of a press release to put across the views of people and groups who act as opinion formers**

⊗ **it may involve sponsorship to link the name of an organisation to a particular event**

A the first two

B the last two

C the first and the last

D all of the above

18 The standard of internal customer service will be raised by all of the following, except :

A a clear understanding amongst the workforce of the organisation's goals

B focusing on major tasks and leaving routine duties

C a clear understanding amongst the workforce of the features of the final product or service

D a philosophy of teamwork

19 All of the following are advantages associated with the wholesaler, except :

A buys in bulk which allows the manufacturer to enjoy production economies of scale

B may help the manufacturer to avoid seasonal fluctuations in output

C speeds up the distribution of perishable items

D generally deals in well-known lines

20 All of the following characteristics are required by a good salesman, except :

A a persuasive personality

B well-developed interpersonal skills

C a dominant manner

D subtle negotiating skills

Index